Rescuing the Bible

Blackwell Manifestos

In this new series major critics make timely interventions to address important concepts and subjects, including topics as diverse as, for example: Culture, Race, Religion, History, Society, Geography, Literature, Literary Theory, Shakespeare, Cinema, and Modernism. Written accessibly and with verve and spirit, these books follow no uniform prescription but set out to engage and challenge the broadest range of readers, from undergraduates to postgraduates, university teachers and general readers – all those, in short, interested in ongoing debates and controversies in the humanities and social sciences.

Already Published

Forthcoming

Rescuing the Bible

Roland Boer

Blackwell
Publishing

© 2007 by Roland Boer

BLACKWELL PUBLISHING
350 Main Street, Malden, MA 02148-5020, USA
9600 Garsington Road, Oxford OX4 2DQ, UK
550 Swanston Street, Carlton, Victoria 3053, Australia

The right of Roland Boer to be identified as the author of this work has been asserted in accordance with the UK Copyright, Designs, and Patents Act 1988.

Designations used by companies to distinguish their products are often claimed as trademarks. All brand names and product names used in this book are trade names, service marks, trademarks, or registered trademarks of their respective owners. The publisher is not associated with any product or vendor mentioned in this book.

This publication is designed to provide accurate and authoritative information in regard to the subject matter covered. It is sold on the understanding that the publisher is not engaged in rendering professional services. If professional advice or other expert assistance is required, the services of a competent professional should be sought.

First published 2007 by Blackwell Publishing Ltd

1   2007

Library of Congress Cataloging-in-Publication Data

Boer, Roland, 1961–
Rescuing the Bible / Roland Boer.
p. cm.—(Blackwell manifestos)
Includes bibliographical references and index.
ISBN 978-1-4051-7021-5 (hardcover : alk. paper)—ISBN 978-1-4051-7020-8 (pbk. : alk. paper) 1. Bible—Criticism, interpretation, etc. I. Title.
BS511.3.B65 2007
220.6—dc22
2007013121

A catalogue record for this title is available from the British Library.

Set in 11.5/13.5pt Bembo
by SPi Publisher Services, Pondicherry, India
Printed and bound in Singapore
by Markono Print Media Pte Ltd

The publisher's policy is to use permanent paper from mills that operate a sustainable forestry policy, and which has been manufactured from pulp processed using acid-free and elementary chlorine-free practices. Furthermore, the publisher ensures that the text paper and cover board used have met acceptable environmental accreditation standards.

For further information on
Blackwell Publishing, visit our website at
www.blackwellpublishing.com

Contents

Preface

I have written this manifesto for general readers who are interested in the current relations between the Bible and politics. I hope that it may also be useful for specialists, but I have put aside the usual chatter of scholarly footnotes, arcane theory and quibbling over minor details of interest to only a few. I do not presume any special relation to the Bible, except that it remains an extremely important political text. The reader may notice here and there that the spirits of Marx and Engels, especially from *The Manifesto of the Communist Party*, are occasionally present.

Unless otherwise indicated, quotations are from the Revised Standard Version, for the simple reason that this translation does not try to smooth over the rougher and unpalatable edges of the Hebrew and Greek texts. Finally, thanks are due to Mark Crees for his invaluable work on this book.

Introduction

My task is to rescue the Bible from the clutches of the religious and political right, its most systematic abusers. It is far too important and too multi-vocal a text to be surrendered to right-wing agendas. As far as the left is concerned, the old divisions of religious left and secular left are no longer workable. So I argue that they should unite in a common front – a 'worldly left' – in order to reclaim and rescue the Bible for radical politics. Fortunately for such a common left, the Bible is so multi-vocal that it is perfectly plausible to draw from it a deep current of revolutionary themes. And it matters not whether those who read the Bible in this way are 'believers' or not.

Theses for a Worldly Left

That, in a nutshell, is the position of this manifesto, but let me put my positions in terms of six theses:

1   Since the old programme of secularism has run aground, I propose a new secularism that sees the entwinement of religion and secularism as necessary and beneficial, that reads the Bible in light of theological suspicion, denounces the abuse of the Bible and fosters liberating readings and uses.
2   Since the religious left has been marginalized and has had the Bible stolen from it, and since the secular left is on the rise, in

order to rescue the Bible we need a politics of alliance between the religious left and the old secular left. I call this alliance the 'worldly left', one that is as wise as serpents and as innocent as doves (Matthew 10:16).

3 Despite the best efforts to impose dominant viewpoints on the Bible, through canonization and interpretation, it remains an unruly and fractious collection of texts. For this reason it is a multivalent collection, both folly to the rich and scandal to the poor (Ernst Bloch).

4 The Bible is too important and too multi-valent a text to be left to the religious right. Thus it is necessary to take sides with the liberatory side of the Bible, and in doing so we denounce the reactionary use and abuse of the Bible, for imperial conquest, oppression of all types and the support of privilege and wealth.

5 Taking the side of liberation, we also need to recover the tradition of revolutionary readings of the Bible.

6 The Bible is one source for a political myth for the worldly left, a political myth that, while keeping in mind the perpetual need for theological suspicion, condemns oppression, imagines a better society and draws deeply on the mythic images of rebellious chaos.

I will say a little more about each thesis, since they encapsulate the main arguments of this book. I begin in the first chapter by proposing that the best context for rescuing the Bible is what I call a 'new secularism'. The reason for such a proposal is that the old programme of secularism in all its different dimensions is flawed and riddled with paradoxes. Despite all the efforts to see the old secularism and religion as implacable opponents, they continue to be entwined in an unholy embrace. The separation of Church and state has become a legal fiction, far removed from the daily politics of states. In biblical scholarship, the supposed distinction between 'scientific' and 'confessional' study of the Bible produces deeply inconsistent scholars who try to keep one foot in both camps. And the process of secularization has run aground with the rise of all manner of personal spiritualities and the return of religion – especially conflicts between the so-called 'religions of the book' – as a major factor in global politics and the 'war on terror'. The answer, I suggest, is not to be found in what some have named 'post-secularism' (the return of spirituality and religion), but in a new secularism. The last part of the chapter outlines what such a new secularism means for the Bible. This new secular approach to the Bible has five features: it recognizes the mutual benefit of the entwinement of religion and secularism; it urges a reading of the Bible in light of theological suspicion in order to block idolatrous readings of the Bible (either as the gods or as human leaders); it denounces abuse of the Bible; it fosters emancipatory readings; and it pursues a politics of alliance between the religious left and the old secular left. These five points of the new secularism really comprise the programme for the rest of the book.

The next chapter develops what I call the 'worldly left' – the alliance between the old secular left and the religious left – as the way to reclaim the Bible. I begin by outlining the background for such an alliance. Thus I trace the way the Bible has been stolen by the religious right. Claiming to be 'Bible-based', the religious right has claimed exclusive ownership of the Bible. By giving into this language, and by focusing its energy on the various causes of identity politics, especially the battles for the ordination of women and the roles of gays and lesbians, the religious left has surrendered the Bible to the religious right. The paradox that just as the religious left is under siege within religious institutions, the secular left is in resurgence, although now in new ways. In this situation, I urge a politics of alliance between the religious left and the old secular left, to the mutual benefit of both. Within that alliance, the Bible can play a central role. Or rather, it has begun to play such a role, for alongside an ever larger number of biblical scholars making use of Marxist methods, we also find an increasing fascination in the midst of the secular left with the political possibilities of the Bible. In light of these developments, I suggest that we should speak of a 'worldly left' as the name for an allied religious and secular left.

The third chapter makes two arguments: the Bible is political-ly multi-valent, and it is an unruly collection of texts that has been colonized and dominated by Synagogue and Church. As far as the multi-valency of the Bible is concerned, two phrases by Ernst Bloch express it very well: while the Bible is 'often a scandal to the poor and not always a folly to the rich' (Bloch 1972: 25), it is also 'the Church's bad conscience' (Bloch 1972: 21). Both observations are true: the Bible has often been and continues to be read as a friend of the rich and powerful *and* it has been and continues to be an inspiration for revolutionary groups seeking to overthrow their rich and powerful oppressors. I explore this political ambivalence of the Bible in two instances: in the debates over Zionism within Judaism; and in the battles over identity politics in the churches. However, a major reason for the multi-valency of the Bible is that it is an unruly collection of texts. In order to show up its unruliness, I retell the story of canonization, which turns out to be nothing less than an effort to suppress and bring to order a fractious rabble of texts. As with any effort to confine undesirables, the texts within the Bible strain to break out and take on very different and often far more interesting identities than the official ones. Needless to say, my position is that the Bible should not remain under the exclusive control of religious institutions and monopolies, for Synagogue and Church are by their very nature overwhelmingly stuffy and conservative. There is no chance in hell that they will become progressive or revolutionary bodies as a whole. They may contain radical, breakaway elements, but, as with the process of canonization, they are either kicked out or roped in.

With such a history behind it, it is no wonder that the religious right finds fertile ground in the Bible for its political and religious programmes. Thus the subject of the fourth chapter is to condemn the (ab)use of the Bible by the religious right. However, by 'abuse' I mean not merely the twisting of biblical texts away from their supposed original meaning, but especially the *use* of those texts that openly support oppression and exploitation – whether in terms of economics, politics, religion, gender, race and so on. It involves, in other words, the *use of abusive texts* from the Bible. Here I am concerned with the Bible in politics, science and education. We find it abused in Australia by the efforts of conservative politicians to construct a myth of a comfortable Christian Australia, untroubled by those annoying interest groups such as feminists, gays and lesbians, indigenous and environmentalist activists and, of course, Muslims. In the USA, we find a sustained effort to slip into the Bible as a superpower, one whose task is to protect an Israel that really becomes an extension of itself. As far as science is concerned, the conflicts between the theories of 'intelligent design' (a slick makeover for an older 'creation science') and evolution increasingly have a profound effect on education, from primary to tertiary levels. Like the current trends in global politics, this is also an abuse of the Bible.

However, the Bible is too multi-valent to be surrendered to the religious and political right, so I turn in the fifth and sixth chapters to ask what a rescued Bible might look like. Such a Bible has two features: a long revolutionary legacy and a basis for a political myth for the worldly left. Thus, in the fifth chapter, I trace that revolutionary legacy. What is it, I ask, about this text that continues to inspire revolutionary movements and trenchant criticisms of political and economic oppression? In order to gain a sense of this tradition, I discuss Thomas Müntzer and the Peasants' Revolt in sixteenth-century Germany; Gerrard Winstanley and the Diggers in seventeenth-century England; liberation theology in our era, especially the guerrilla priest Camilo Torres; and then the long history of religious socialism. Perhaps the most intriguing feature is that secular revolutionary movements have also drawn from the Bible, and so I consider both Georges Sorel and Ernst Bloch.

In the sixth chapter I offer a few suggestions for building a biblical political myth that may be of use to a worldly left. I speak of myth quite deliberately, and especially of political myth. And the reason is not merely that the Bible deals in mythology, but also that myth is an extraordinarily powerful political medium. Some of the ingredients of such a political myth may be found in the vast biblical storehouse of progressive and revolutionary images, metaphors and stories. There are three elements in the proposed political myth: the repeated condemnations of economic and social exploitation and oppression, the metaphors of a better social and economic order, and the deep theme of rebellious chaos and disorder.

1

The New Secularism

First Thesis: Since the old programme of secularism has run aground, I propose a new secularism that sees the entwinement of religion and secularism as necessary and beneficial, that reads the Bible in light of theological suspicion, denounces the abuse of the Bible and fosters liberating readings and uses.

This chapter explores what the first thesis means in some detail. It sets up the context for rescuing the Bible in terms of the collapse of the old secularism, the false hopes of 'post-secularism' and the possibilities of what I call the new secularism.

Introduction

In late 1999 I taught a class entitled 'Culture, Religion and Spirituality'. Such a course had never been taught before at this particular place, the University of Western Sydney, but at the first class the students flooded in and I found myself with more than I could handle. In particular, there were two surprises in store for me. The first was more personal: I suddenly realized that I has slipped into another generation, for these students were the age of my eldest children. The true meaning of those things I had been denying, such as the wombat nose, sprouting ears, and an increasing chrome dome, was now revealed to me.

6

More importantly, however, was the fact that virtually none of the students in the course would admit to being religious. If they were anything, it was spiritual. No one, apart from a stray fundamentalist or two who had wandered into the class by mistake, read their Bibles. But they read and did a great many other things. There was the Satanist who gave a tutorial telling us how nice Marilyn Manson really is. Or the sports freak, who told us she felt spiritual when her stomach muscles ached from too many sit-ups. Then there were the crystals passed around another tutorial group; 'feel how warm they are', we were instructed, as we heard how they help calm and orient oneself in the morning. In another tutorial, a student told us about the spirituality of the *Matrix* films, showing snippets of the film from a badly pirated copy that must have been made with a hand-held camera in the cinema. Perhaps my favourite was a presentation, held off until the last day and given a little nervously. After a last drag on a menthol cigarette the student pulled a pile of books out of his bag in order to bolster his position. He then proceeded to explain – with abundant 'proof' – how all the great religious leaders were actually from a superior civilization that happened to live on one of the comets that passed the Earth every few centuries. Moses, Zoroaster, Jesus, Mohammed and the Buddha had all leapt to earth for a time, passed on their wisdom recorded in the various scriptures, and then rejoined their galactic home as it moved on. When I asked him how they had managed that small problem of leaping through space onto Earth and back again, the reply was disarmingly simple: they are superior to us, aren't they?

My experience with this class raises in an acute form the topic of this chapter: the relation of the Bible to secularism, post-secularism and what I will call the 'new secularism'. In particular, the question I faced was why it had become perfectly acceptable, cool even, to be spiritual. It was certainly not what I had assumed was the status quo: not that long ago, if you showed a tendency to meditate and hum the sacred syllable, 'om', or if you actually went to church and read the Bible, you were a 'weirdo', part of a fading minority, and definitely not cool. What had changed? I wondered. Why was secularism on the retreat after a century and a half of a somewhat rocky march forward?

7

So in the chapter that follows I need to make a detour through the issues of secularism and post-secularism before returning in the second half to consider the impact of these developments on the Bible and how it might be read.

The Paradoxes of Secularism

As for my discoveries in the 'Culture, Religion and Spirituality' course, I soon found a term for the development of all manner of spiritualities, a development that had somehow escaped me, trapped as I was at the time in an insular church-based theological college. It is post-secularism. But before I discuss that, a few words on secularism are in order. Although I am usually wary of etymologies that trace the meaning of a word back to its Latin or Greek origin, occasionally the exercise is useful. 'Secularism' derives from the Latin term *saeculum* (adjective, *saecularis*); it means an age, a generation, or the spirit of the age. The basic meaning of secularism (it was coined by George Holyoake around 1850 after a short stint in prison for blasphemy) draws from this Latin sense; *it designates a system of thought, indeed a way of living that draws its terms purely from this age and from this world.* That is the positive sense of the term. Of course, it has an implied negative, namely that secularism does not draw its reference point from something beyond this world, whether that is a god or the gods above, or a time in the future, or indeed a sacred text such as the Bible that talks about both.[1]

If secularism designates a certain way of living and thinking, then its related term – secularization – deals with the process by which secularism comes about. More specifically, secularization is the long process in which the key reference points for the everyday workings of a capitalist society focus on this age and this world and not any world beyond. With a few bumps and hiccoughs on the way, secularization has generally been understood as an inexorable process. One by one, social assumptions concerning everything from sexuality to food have been shifting their focus away from religious authority.

These are the basic senses of secularism and secularization with which I work. However, there are some derivatives or secondary features of these terms that I will discuss briefly: secularism as an anti-religious programme; the nature of intellectual inquiry, especially biblical studies; and the separation of Church and state. Most significantly, I want to highlight the fact that each secondary feature has a number of problems and paradoxes. Finally, I consider the paradox of secularization itself.

Anti-religious secularism

The problem with a term such as secularism is that its sense has slipped to mean anything that is opposed to supernatural religion. Secularism then becomes another word for atheism. This slippage and confusion of the term was made quite clear to me in the story of a now distant friend. He had been appointed as the inaugural lecturer in studies in religion at a rural university. On enrolment day, he dutifully took up his seat in the enrolment hall, seeking to enlist the odd student who wanted to take his only course for that year, 'An Introduction to Religious Experience'. In a few minutes, a stout grey-bearded lecturer from another discipline walked up to his desk and boomed out so that all could hear, 'Are you the new religious studies lecturer?' My friend replied in the affirmative. 'Are you religious?' asked the other lecturer. This time the reply was negative. 'I don't believe you', said the man. 'This studies in religion you're supposed to teach – it's just a cover for religious proselytizing. Religion has no place in a secular university'. The other lecturer thumped off to his desk as my friend pondered what he had walked into.

This bearded lecturer had made the popular confusion of secularism with a non-religious or indeed an anti-religious stance. However, we can distinguish this sense – the anti-religious one – from the basic sense of secularism rather easily. If secularism means a system of thought and a way of life that is based in this world and this age, then the anti-religious sense is derivative and not crucial to its meaning.[2] The catch is that too often implications like this one are understood to be *the* meaning of secularism. Yet the anti-religious position *may* follow from secularism, it may even be an implication of it, but it is secondary to the meaning of secularism itself. Too soon problems arise with the anti-religious position. If we take such a position, then secularism becomes confused with atheism, which is itself a religious position. It is an old point, but the denial or rejection of a god or gods would not be possible if there were no religions. Formally, atheism is no different from the many other religious commitments one might make.

Further, there are a good many people who are religious secularists and who see no contradiction in holding both religion and secularism together. What they mean by this is that secularism is the basis for religious tolerance, arguing that secularism was an effort to deal with the religious conflict between Roman Catholics and Protestants in Europe. No one religion should lord it over another, and the only way to ensure such tolerance is to insist on a secular society that favours none. Again, this is an implication or one of the outcomes of the basic sense of secularism.

Biblical studies

As far as intellectual disciplines are concerned, secularism means that they must operate in a secular manner. Here the catchwords are 'science' and 'reason'. A discipline is 'scientific' and operates according to principles of 'reason' if it makes use of evidence and develops its hypotheses and theories on the basis of such evidence, not on any divine revelation. As for the Bible, even theology and biblical studies must be scientific in order to be disciplines of any value. One still hears claims that biblical studies is a scientific discipline, concerned with the hard data of textual manuscripts, history, archaeological artefacts and other sundry pieces. Indeed, some claim that biblical studies has been a secular discipline for well over a century, and that this tradition is well worth fighting for over against the return of faith-based readings. What is meant by this claim is that when biblical scholars deal with the history of the text – its gradual development into the final text we have now – and the history behind the text, or indeed the history of interpretation of the text, they do not count divine forces or influences as viable historical categories. God or the gods are matters of faith and not scholarship.

At this point we really face a paradox, if not outright confusion: a good many, if not the majority, of biblical scholars carry out their secular 'scientific' research to the exclusion of matters of religious faith. Yet a good many of them also attend a church or synagogue at the weekend. To top it off, the students they teach, whether in secular universities or in theological colleges, are often training for some form of ministry. This is an old paradox, and I am not the first to point it out: many biblical scholars live double lives, one of secular scholarship and the other of a personal life of faith, and never the twain shall meet. This contradiction may take a number of forms: in Europe we find secular theology faculties in the state universities, engaged in scientific research, who train people in secular biblical studies to be priests and ministers. In the United States, where such theology faculties cannot exist in state universities, but where 'divinity schools' operate in many private universities, many biblical scholars try to keep their objective scholarship separate from their personal lives of faith. And in Australia, where most biblical studies is taught in theological colleges, the biblical studies lecturer will move from teaching, for example, the theory of various sources for the Gospels, to preaching from the same Gospels at the weekly chapel service. Nothing to my mind shows how much the old programme of secularism is flawed. In light of this confusing situation, it has become a commonplace to assume, especially by those outside biblical studies, that the proper place for biblical studies is a theological college or theology department.

Church and state

A further troubled derivative of secularism is the separation of Church and state. Perhaps the most discussed version of such a separation may be found in the United States, where the relevant section of the First Amendment to the Constitution reads: 'Congress shall make no law respecting an establishment of religion, or prohibiting the free exercise thereof'. Initially a response to the established Church of England, especially after the American War of Independence, it has come to be interpreted as any act by the Congress and the legislature that favours one religion over another with the possible outcome that such a religion may become established. In practice, this really means Christianity and shows up with monotonous regularity in the area of state-funded education. The Bible is not to be taught, prayer is not appropriate and one cannot teach religious doctrines in state schools. As we will see in Chapter Four, a major area of conflict in state education in the USA concerns the efforts to have 'intelligent design' taught as a scientific alternative to evolutionary theory. The proponents of intelligent design keep coming up against the First Amendment; the courts keep deciding that intelligent design is a religious, not a scientific, theory, and therefore has no place in public schools. As a result, the First Amendment has come to be interpreted as an effort to restrict the promotion of religion by the state.

However, in the United States the separation of Church and state has become something of a legal fiction. The more strictly the courts apply the First Amendment, the more pervasive religion becomes in public life. An external observer cannot help noticing that religion saturates public life in the USA: the founding myth of the escape from oppression to a land of freedom is drawn from the story of the Exodus and the Promised Land; presidents must be openly Christian, they make decisions with religious concerns in mind, most recently on the questions of sex education and stem-cell research; voting patterns follow religious lines, and, especially in the Bible Belt, there is a sharp polarization over religion. One is either passionately Christian or passionately atheist.

I am tempted to argue for an equation: the sharper the separation between Church and state, the more the two mingle with each other. The obverse of this equation may be found in the countries that do have an established church, such as Denmark, Sweden, Norway and England, where we find that secularism is far advanced indeed. However, this equation doesn't hold in all situations, as France shows all too clearly. With its doctrine of *laïcité*, the separation of Church and state in France is much more deeply entrenched. The government must not support any religious position, including atheism. The First Article of the French Constitution reads: '*La France est une République, unie, indivisible, laïque et sociale*'. Indeed, it is distinctly un-French to display one's religion openly, especially if one is a politician or public servant. Yet a problem, and controversial one at that, has arisen in France: that of the *hijab* (literally 'modesty'), a covering or veil, worn by Muslim women. In line with the principle of *laïcité*, the French government passed a law on 15 March 2004 that bans overtly religious dress and signs in public or state-run schools. These items include Sikh turbans, Christian crosses, Jewish skullcaps and of course the *hijab* for Muslim women, or more specifically the *khimer* or headscarf that some Muslim women wear. While the law does not state what items of clothing or signs are to be banned, the timing suggests that the issue that sparked the law was the *hijab* or *khimer*. This has become an impossible issue to resolve: allowing the *hijab* would be an exercise of religious toleration and freedom; banning the *hijab* confirms the non-religious nature of French public institutions. Both positions are consistent with the separation of Church and state, and yet both cannot exist together.

I am about to move onto the third derivative of secularism, namely the process of secularization, but there is one last example of the paradox concerning the separation of Church and state I would like to raise – Turkey. Ever since Atatürk, the first President of the Republic of Turkey, disestablished Islam as the state religion in 1924, the separation of Church and state has been fundamental in Turkey. Government departments and employees, including schools and universities, must operate without influence from the Sunni Muslim majority. Yet in Turkey the paradox I have been tracing shows up in a different way. Under the auspices of the Department of Religious Affairs, Islam is watched closely: while the state supports mosques through taxes and subsidies, the content of sermons, statements and views must avoid political content, and, as in France, all female state employees are banned from wearing the *hijab*. The state also restricts any independent religious communities and religious schools. What we have here is a situation analogous to the established church in some western European countries, and yet that recognition, even to the point of providing state funds, is a means of ensuring that Islam and its institutions do not interfere in the political realm. It is an ingenious if highly paradoxical solution.

Secularization

My last search for paradoxes is with secularization itself – the historical process in which life in capitalist society has shifted its points of reference to this world and not any world beyond. Of course, the nature of this historical process is hotly debated, but what I find intriguing is that even in the most secularized societies, there has been a sharp recovery of the idea that 'Western' society is based on biblical and Christian values, that the Bible is its founding document, if you will. I am saying nothing new by pointing out that this recovery has much to do with the perceived threat of Islam. Confident, robust and open societies across Western Europe once brought in workers from the Middle East, most of them Muslims, to do the jobs that no-one else wanted to do. These people settled, brought their families, had children, and today the countries that first actively encouraged these immigrants have become fearful. Now, I have little sympathy with the fear of a so-called 'terrorist' attack, since I have about as much chance of being knocked off my bicycle or being stung to death by a bee as I have of dying in a bomb attack. The threat may be largely a fiction, but the fear is real – even if it is the manifestation of a host of other fears such as climate change or economic collapse. And in response to that fear we find assertions of the essentially Christian nature of the West by people who have not had a religious thought or feeling from the moment they were born.

At one level, this reassertion of the Christian roots of the West is a statement of the obvious. Indeed, another version of secularization is that it involved the gradual process of emptying the theological content from central ideas, such as justice, love, authority and community, and refilling them with a secular content. Justice is then not based on the Ten Commandments but on the needs of human beings to live together (respecting private property of course); love is not a divine quality that Jesus commands in the New Testament but a necessary human process for reproduction, and so on. What has happened then is that the recovery of the idea of a Christian West is a recovery of the half-forgotten basis of Western society. Secularization becomes a veneer for a deeper Christian – or as some like to call it, a Judaeo-Christian – heritage. The story is all too familiar: the Ten Commandments are the basis of the rule of law, respect for private property and for one's parents; the command of Jesus to love your neighbour as yourself, as the second greatest commandment, is the basis for human society, of which the Church is the ideal; the call to follow Jesus is the basis of the idea of a vocation or calling to a profession; and so on and so on.

This recovery is but the first sign of a contradiction at the heart of secularization. The second is that the very idea of a 'Christian West' is a fantasy that has been perpetuated for hundreds of years on the basis that the West is different from the East, especially the Muslim East. That fantasy trades on the idea that 'the West' was somehow established by the widely perceived fear of Islam (or rather, the Turks) throughout the Middle Ages. Rather, the West is unimaginable without Islam, for the idea of 'the West' began with the expulsion of what made it possible in the first place: the Moors in Spain in the fifteenth century. Several million Muslims and Jews were either forced to convert to Catholicism, or flee, in a programme that would now be called ethnic cleansing. Even so, hundreds of thousands of resolutely Catholic *Moriscos* – 'Spaniards' of (mixed) Muslim ancestry – were expelled as well, including priests, monks and nuns. The capture of the last Muslim outpost of Grenada in the auspicious year of 1492 marks the beginning of a long process by which Europe appropriated Muslim learning, dragged itself out of an intellectual and cultural backwater, and identified itself as Christian and West. Today, the more the ruling classes try to marginalize and demonize Islam, the more it becomes clear that the West relies on Islam for its very identity (see further Boer and Abraham in press).

Conclusion

So much for secularism and secularization: I have done enough to show that it is riven with problems and paradoxes. In fact, I would suggest that the old programme of secularism is deeply flawed. The paradox of anti-religious secularism is that it is a religious position; the separation of Church and state seems to produce a whole range of unofficial involvements of the state in religion; the development of an apparently scientific biblical studies leads to a scholarly paradox; and in the midst of the process of secularization we find a contradictory assertion that secularized Western societies are in fact Christian societies, which is itself a fantasy that conceals the Muslim roots of the Christian West. What are we to do? Do we just give in and admit that it is well-nigh impossible to separate the secular and the religious, the scientific and the biblical?

Post-secularism

I would suggest that we need to think about secularism rather differently. The problems I have outlined above do not mean the end of secularism as such, or at least that secularism is a sham. Rather, the critical perspective on secularism that I have outlined briefly is a sign of something rather different, namely what is increasingly called post-secularism. I want to emphasize two features of this post-secularism: the first is the reassessment and critical perspective on secularism, especially the realization that secularism really is the flip side of religion; the second is the explosion of a host of spiritualities and, more lately, religion itself.[3] In other words, the 'post' of post-secularism has both critical and historical senses. Since I have discussed the critical sense of post-secularism in the preceding section, here I will focus on the second, more historical dimension.

Let me go back to my class on 'Culture, Religion and Spirituality' where I came to terms with my advancing years and the new spiritualities sprouting up everywhere. These were students in a secular university, one that has no formal programme in theology, let alone biblical studies, and yet here were scores of students asserting their relatively new-found spiritualities, all the way from crystals to comet-bound saviours. These students were my first-hand experience with one aspect of what has come to be called post-secularism.

The rise of spiritualities

Something has indeed changed. We need to be careful at this point, for there are two phases to this historical change. The first is the rise of a host of essentially private spiritualities, and the second is the return of religion to the centre of the public, global stage. These two, the sprouting spiritualities and the return of religion, mark distinct moments in the unfolding of post-secularism. As far as spiritualities are concerned, the crucial period is the 1960s and 1970s when hippie culture and the alternative lifestyle movement began the search for alternative religious practices that had been buried under the dominant culture. Wicca and the occult more generally, indigenous religions, astrology, various forms of Buddhism, the Tao and Hinduism all became viable sources for such alternative spiritualities. But as is the way with such movements within capitalism, all too soon these spiritualities became big business. Indeed, they seemed all too suited to capitalism, with their focus on the private individual and the inner life. One might exhibit that glowing eye of the fanatic, or perhaps the strange inner calm that was more than the effect of laxatives, but above all it was a private affair. Further, sundry practitioners sprang up like spiritual entrepreneurs, selling insights into one's hidden life, the future, the alignment of one's poles and what have you. It became chic to have crystals and perhaps a pyramid in one's apartment, and to consult the stars and Tarot over morning coffee, and all of these spiritual accessories could be bought at a market fair, or your local incense-laden shop. By the 1990s one could be *spiritual* in all manner of senses, but God – or rather, the spirits – forbid that one should be *religious*. No-one wanted to be religious any more, since religion had that reek of moth-eaten robes and empty religious buildings, whether Jewish synagogues, Christian churches or Muslim mosques. Religion had become the bogey term, that from which nearly everyone recoiled in institutional horror. To be spiritual, on the other hand, meant being free to pick and choose from supposed ancient practices or from any of the new forms that sprang up daily. And if you did read your Bible, it was for some kinky spiritual reason rather than anything as straightforward as conventional belief.

Eclectic, private, free from political as well as institutional taint, these spiritualities seemed to run against that fundamental tenet of secularism, namely the need to refer only to this age and this world. Why, people began wondering, did all these spiritualities spring up when secularization was everywhere dominant? An all too easy answer trotted out once too often is that our (post-)modern, materialistic world does not provide spiritual answers. You still hear this tired old reason spouted by those who feel that the ecological 'crisis' is a spiritual crisis. People hunger for spiritual realities, they say, for a deeper spiritual truth. As politely as possible, let me say that this is rubbish. Rather, the rise of spirituality is a major – I hesitate to write 'first' – sign of the tensions within secularism and the beginnings of post-secularism.

On the other hand, spirituality fits perfectly well with another feature of secularism: any spiritual or religious belief should be a private affair and should not be shouted from the rooftops, or worse still, affect one's exercise of public office. Whether one dances in a circle at the winter solstice, or feels the movements of planetary bodies at every moment of the day, or attends a Roman Catholic mass at least twice a week, or indeed reads one's Bible for devotional or spiritual reasons, these practices should not influence one's life in business or government or education. The new spiritualities obeyed this rule of secularism rather well. Private spirituality was fine; institutional religion was not.

The return of religion

At least that was the case until those planes flew into the twin towers of the World Trade Centre in New York on 11 September 2001. Since then religion has certainly been in, especially the religions of the book.

18

Or at least it has been at the forefront of public policy and the public imagination. Soon we encountered the rhetoric of 'axis of evil' and the 'evil empire' invoked by the President of the United States in order to describe Iraq, Iran and North Korea, and then quite specifically to designate Muslim majority states. Mr Bush was then called 'the devil' himself in response, not merely by Muslim leaders but by the President of Venezuela, Hugo Chávez, who is himself a Christian with a distinct liking for liberation theology.

One after another the stories came to light: George W. Bush took part in Bible study groups at the White House, sought divine guidance, and felt that God had told him to invade Iraq. Pat Robertson, one of the religious right's major leaders in the USA, called on the USA to assassinate Venezuela's president, Hugo Chávez. And Christian Zionists became increasingly influential in US policies towards the Middle East. Christian Zionism, a standard position among the religious right, especially in the United States, may be defined as Christian support for the Zionist programme of the establishment and maintenance of the state of Israel. In a nutshell, it holds that the key events of the end of history, as interpreted through the New Testament, will take place quite soon in modern Israel. These events involves the arrival of the anti-Christ, Jesus's return to destroy the forces of evil in the final battle of Armageddon, and then his rule on earth, all of which will take place in Israel.

Of course, the Bible is central in the Christian Zionist programme. They string together a number of disparate passages to come up with a strangely coherent narrative. Thus they take the passages from the Hebrew Bible (Old Testament), especially those concerning the promise of a full occupation of the land of Canaan (Genesis 15:18–21, 17:7–8, Numbers 34:1–12), as referring to the present day 'return' of the Jews to Palestine. The first moment of the end, the 'Rapture', comes from 1 Thessalonians 4:15–17, especially verse 17: 'then we who are alive, who are left, shall be caught up together with them in the clouds to meet the Lord in the air'. Matthew 24:40–1 also helps: 'Then two men will be in the field; one is taken and one is left. Two women will be grinding at the mill; one is taken and one is left'.

Another important passage is 1 Thessalonians 5:1–11, with its depiction of the day of the Lord coming 'like a thief in the night'. This Rapture is nothing other than the moment when all true believers will suddenly be whisked away into heaven, all at the same moment. It marks the beginning of the end times.

Throw in the seven seals from Revelation (6:1–17 and 8:1–5) and you get the seven years of tribulation after the Rapture, with Matthew 24, Mark 13 and Luke 21 helping out with the term 'Tribulation'. Paul's words in Romans 11:11–27, especially his desire 'to make some of my fellow Jews jealous, and thus save some of them' (verse 14), becomes the prophecy of a part of the Jews. The exact number to be converted comes from Revelation 7:1–8 with its mention of 'a hundred and forty-four thousand sealed, out of every tribe of the sons of Israel' (verse 4). The rest will be annihilated. The battle of Armageddon comes from Revelation 16:16, and the final conflict between the armies of Jesus and the Beast appears in Revelation 17:13–14: 'These [the ten kings] are of one mind and give over their power and authority to the beast; they will make war on the Lamb, and the Lamb will conquer them, for he is Lord of lords and King of kings, and those with him are called and chosen and faithful' (see also Daniel 7 and 11).

In sum, after the anti-Christ (in Babylon) and seven years of tribulation, Armageddon in Israel will be the scene of the final battle, after which will come 1,000 years of peace. Jerry Falwell, another leader among the religious right in the USA, puts it well. Preaching at the outbreak of the first Iraq war, Falwell told us what to expect when the end comes, which it will, sooner rather than later:

> While the dead are buried over a seven-month period of time during the Kingdom Age that has just began, our Lord Jesus with the Saints will sit down upon the Throne of David in Jerusalem and for one thousand years will rule in perfect peace upon the earth … God still has one thousand and seven years of use for this planet. The seven-year Tribulation period, the thousand-year Kingdom Age … (cited in Harding 1994: 73)

There is one small catch if you happen to be a Jew: all the Jews who refuse to convert to Christianity will simply be wiped out in the battle to end all battles. This problem hasn't escaped Jewish commentators, such as Gershom Gorenberg, who states, 'The Jews die or convert … I can't feel very comfortable with the affections of somebody who looks forward to that scenario … it's a five-act play in which the Jews disappear in the fourth act …'. (Simon 2002).

In Australia, vilifications of Muslims by politicians became the new version of anti-Semitism: Islamophobia found expression in caricatures of a violent and misogynist religion hell-bent on destroying Western culture. One after another, politicians of all stripes tried to outdo each other in the new game of Muslim-baiting, all in the name of a biblically based Christian heritage. For example, Peter Costello, the reactionary Treasurer of the Australian Federal Government recently said: 'Before entering a mosque visitors are asked to take off their shoes … This is a sign of respect. If you have a strong objection to walking in your socks, don't enter the mosque. Before becoming an Australian you will be asked to subscribe to certain values. If you have strong objections to those values, don't come to Australia' (Garnaut 2006). Not one to miss out on a chance to go even lower, the Prime Minister, John Howard, has picked on the perceived oppression of women in Islam, signalled by the *burqa*, or full body covering (see Farouque 2006), and what he sees as jihad-mongering extremists. Indeed, Howard finds the whole community of immigrant Muslims a problem: 'It is not a problem that we have ever faced with other immigrant communities who become easily absorbed by Australia's mainstream' (Schubert 2006). For their part, the Exclusive Brethren hired a private detective to dig up dirt on the husband of New Zealand's prime minister (Helen Clark), releasing a story that suggested he was gay. The substantial contributions of the Brethren to the reactionary National Party, their expensive advertising in favour of John Howard and against the Greens in Australia also came to light.

On it goes. However, I am at risk of a common mistake – attributing too much to the destruction of the World Trade Centre, or '9/11' as it is often called (recognizing Osama Bin Laden's punning reference to the USA emergency phone number in the timing of the attack). It is not so much the cause of the return of religion into the political and cultural spheres of life, but rather the convenient signal of a change. And that change is the second phase of the rise of post-secularism: in its first phase we found essentially private spiritualities sprouting forth all over the place; now, it is a very public and political religion that has returned. I need to be careful at this point, for it is not all religions that are equally in focus: Islam, Christianity and to a lesser extent Judaism are the religions in question – the so-called 'religions of the book'.

Not only has religion returned to the stage, not only have church, synagogue and mosque become the topic of urgent conversation and political policy (under the propaganda term of 'terrorism'), but the Bible finds itself blinking in the harsh glare of the spotlights. All too accustomed to the quiet corners of ageing religious institutions, used to the pious attention of students training for the priesthood and ministries of different churches and synagogues, used to the contemplative murmur of those strange creatures, biblical scholars, the Bible is now behind the microphones and cameras, forced to answer prickly questions from inquisitive journalists. Is the Bible really a violent text? Is it misogynist, or homophobic? Is it the basis of 'family values' or of private property? Is it an oppressive text or a liberating one? Or is it the fount of Western culture and 'democracy'? Do you need to believe in God to be able to understand it? Indeed, things have changed for students of the Bible. In the 1980s and 1990s it was quaint, at the most, to be a biblical scholar, but one was certainly not in demand. If you wanted a job teaching the Bible, and not merely droning on to a dwindling number of grey heads on a Saturday or Sunday morning, then a rare job or two might have opened up every decade. Or one might eke out an existence in some disguise or other, such as religion scholar, or parish minister or priest, perhaps a scholar of literature or the sociology of religion, or even a radio announcer (not a few have taken this path in Australia). Now, however, that esoteric training in languages, ancient history and the interpretation of a motley collection of texts that some claim as sacred scripture is in demand. The suspicion abounds, among politicians, commentators, policy makers and newspaper editors, that the Bible may indeed have something to do with the current climate of global fear. What exactly does the Bible have to do with the 'New World Order' (remember that phrase?) where supposedly democratic states become increasingly totalitarian while using the lame excuse of 'security'?

Post-secularism, then, has two features: a critical perspective on secularism itself, and the historical shift to a renewed interest in the spiritual life and religion as such. In what follows I will argue that we need a 'new secularism', particularly with regard to the Bible. Tossed about in the currents and waves of spirituality and religion, the Bible faces a problem: if we declare that secular biblical studies is an oxymoron, then do we allow all manner of spiritual, religious and political readings as perfectly acceptable?

The New Secularism

In response to this situation, I argue that we need a new secularism, with particular reference to the Bible. The new secularism *both* recognizes the importance of this age and this world *and* offers a sustained criticism of it. This new secularism has the following five points:

1   It begins with the recognition that religion and secularism are entwined like two strands of a rope and asserts that this is to the benefit of both.
2   In light of the paradox of witch-hunts, it operates by means of a theological suspicion that seeks to read the Bible neither as a sacred text nor 'merely' as profane literature. Theological suspicion leads to the following three points.
3   Suspicious of both religious and secular (ab)use of the Bible, it identifies and denounces such (ab)use.
4   Where possible, it fosters emancipatory uses of the Bible, whether religious or secular.
5   It seeks a politics of alliance.

The entwinement of the Bible and secularism

Let me begin with a parable. Once, a group of scientists – physicists, chemists and biologists – set out to climb a particularly difficult and high mountain. They have all the necessary equipment with them, such as ropes, high-grip boots, tents, thermal clothing and high-energy food. For what seems like an eternity they climb, at times quickly, more often slowly, and at times they come to a dead end and must backtrack in order to find a better way upward. On the way they have their disagreements, threaten to break up the group, and then learn to co-operate with one another. Finally, they come to the last part of the mountain, a particularly rocky and steep section that requires a concerted effort from the weary and dirty scientists. With one last heave, they climb over the ledge, and what do they see? A group of hoary old men, with one or two women, well rugged up against the cold, sit around a campfire. The scientists stagger over to the group and ask, 'What are you doing here?' 'Oh, we're biblical scholars', says one of the group. 'With a few theologians', says another, 'and we've been here for ages'.

Others have told this parable, although probably not in this form. Its point is obvious: scientists still pursue ultimate questions that have been the preserve of biblical scholars and theologians, such as the origin of life or of the universe itself, or the workings of universal laws; or they seek to uncover puzzles and paradoxes, all in order to understand better the world, and indeed the universe. Usually, this story or ones like it are told to unmask the objective pretensions of science. Is not science the ultimate expression of secularism in the old sense? If we can merely show that these pretensions are at heart religious or biblical, then we have shown up science as a secularized religion.

My point is quite different: science, as the flagship of secularism, cannot separate itself from religious questions.[4] Rather than saying, to paraphrase the Marquis de Sade,[5] 'One last effort, my dear scientists, in order to be truly secular, for you are not secular just yet', I would rather say that we should begin any consideration of the new secularism from the recognition of the inseparability of secularism and religion. Fellow travellers they are, but also far more. It is not merely the case that this entwinement is a fact of life; rather it is actually *to the benefit of both*. Rather than resigning themselves to the presence of an unwelcome partner, they gain strength from one another.

The problem with witches, or, theological suspicion

In 1234, the Church's Inquisition burnt its first witch. In 1782 the last witch was executed in Switzerland. During that time somewhere around 40,000 witches were hunted down and put to death. Initially, the problem was eradicating heresy, and witches occasionally came under suspicion by the Inquisition. However, from approximately 1450, waves of mass hysteria swept Europe until the end of the seventeenth century. Following the biblical injunctions, 'You shall not permit a sorceress to live' (Exodus 22:18) and 'A man or a woman who is a medium or a wizard shall be put to death' (Leviticus 20:27), witches were put on trial, tortured and killed.[6]

The problem with witch-hunts is that they produce ever more witches. You are never quite sure if you have managed to eradicate the last one, so there is always at least one more. The situation is not unlike the current hysteria over terrorism and Islam. But it is also the problem with secularism, or at least the form of it that sought to eradicate religion. There is always going to be one more theological skeleton in the closet, one more scientist who has that whiff of biblical religion, one more politician who tries to enact policies that agree with his or her religious belief, one more biblical scholar who sneaks religious commitment into the interpretation of the Bible.

In order to avoid this situation where religion and secularism perpetually chase each other's tails, we require what I would like to call 'theological suspicion' when reading the Bible. I draw the idea from Theodor Adorno (1973), although I have given it a name and a distinct practice. Theological suspicion means that *we should be perpetually on our guard against the theological history, content and use of the Bible.* The Bible is not merely one text in the Western canon that can be treated like any other book. Rather, what we need is an approach that accounts, in the very process of interpretation, for the theological effects of the text. This is partly due to the institutional context of Synagogue and Church in which the Bible has been passed down, but also due to its content. It does after all talk about God and the gods, people who do or do not do what God says, and so forth. In other words, I am suggesting a way of reading that *takes into account and critiques the theological underpinnings* of the Bible and the discipline whose business it is to interpret the Bible, namely, biblical criticism. Similarly, we need a way of holding Church and Synagogue responsible for their domination and (ab)use of the Bible; for their continued rejection in many quarters of people due to gender, sexuality, race and class. We must not let these religious institutions off the hook.

There is one further point from Adorno, who is always worth a reread. He was particularly scathing of secular theology. By this term he meant those systems of thought that believed they had managed to exorcise theology from their own workings. Too many philosophical systems have attempted to laicize or secularize theology; that is, they have taken theological terms, emptied them of their theological content and then refilled them with secular content. What happens is that theology has a knack of sneaking in the back door in even more powerful forms. Now, Adorno has in mind philosophy, but the same applies to the study of the Bible. It is not merely the case that biblical scholars cannot keep their lives of faith separate from their secular scholarship; rather, the attempt to separate the two makes the effect of religious commitment on the scholarship even more powerful since it is now hidden. The same applies to politicians: a politician may have a private belief that the Bible is the Word of God and that he or she should follow its teachings. However, in public life this politician will seek to make decisions without obvious recourse to the Bible, giving other reasons for opposing abortion or gay couples or stem-cell research. Unnamed and unacknowledged, the Bible is even more powerful in this politician's public life than if it were openly proclaimed. This force of the Bible, generated by a belief that it is sacred scripture and yet hidden, is what theological suspicion seeks to unmask. There are two implications of theological suspicion: the need to denounce (ab)use and to foster emancipatory readings.

Denouncing (ab)use

The new secularism undertakes the task of identifying and denouncing (ab)use of the Bible, especially in politics and society. Let me make it perfectly clear what I mean by (ab)use of the Bible. I do not mean abuse in terms of heresy. That is, 'abuse' does not mean deviation from some supposed doctrinal truth, some perversion of the true meaning of the text. By (ab)use I mean the use of texts in order to dominate, oppress and denigrate others. Now there are plenty of texts in the Bible that can do this without much twisting or interpreting away from some legendary true meaning. Indeed, this type of direct abuse, without perversion of what the text says, is the worst of all. In other words, biblical texts can be *used* for the purpose of *abuse* without too much fancy footwork – hence my use of parentheses in '(ab)use'.

There are a number of ways such a denouncing of (ab)use may be done. I follow a more systematic approach in Chapter Four, but we also find distinctly playful ways of doing so. One such possibility is the outrageous 'Brick Testament' (www.thebricktestament.com). Drawing on many of the biblical stories in both Hebrew Bible and New Testament, the stories are illustrated using Lego reconstructions. These reconstructions are then photographed, and on the website and in the books they form a series of stills with biblical texts beneath them. Without commentary, they tell the stories as they are. Each story is rated according to the categories N (nudity), S (sexual content), V (violence) and C (cursing). My favourites would have to be 'The Second Circumcision' (Joshua 5:2–8), 'When to Stone Your Whole Family' (Deuteronomy 13:6–10), 'How Long to Hang Somebody' (Deuteronomy 21:23) and the 'Instructions on Marriage' (1 Corinthians 7:1–9).

However, by means of small twists in the reconstructed scenes the Brick Testament manages to show how abusive such texts can be. You will have to look for yourself in order to see what they are, but let me give one example. In the story, 'When to Stone Your Whole Family', the opening scene has beneath it the quotation, 'If your brother, or your son or daughter, or your beloved wife tries to secretly entice you, telling you to go and worship other gods, gods of people living near you, or far from you, or anywhere on earth, do not listen to him' (Deut. 13:6–8). In the Lego reconstruction we see a family, with a father sitting down reading the newspaper. His wife says 'Jesus is Lord'. A character who appears to be his brother says, 'Hey Jon, what say you come worship Jesus with us'. And his daughter says, 'C'mon dad'. For this they must be stoned, and the next scene has the father throwing stones at them, with the quotation, 'You must kill them. Show them no pity. And your hand must strike the first blow' (Deut. 13:8–9).

Created by a laconic and self-titled 'Reverend' Brendan Powell Smith, the Brick Testament quietly brings out all of the tensions of the Bible, especially its obnoxious and toxic texts, but also its better ones. Above all, it is one exhibit in the new secularism, created by an atheist, but one who is clearly fascinated with the Bible and yet who does not subscribe to any religious belief concerning it.

Emancipatory uses

At this point, I would like to invoke Ernst Bloch's (1972) old point: the pernicious and damaging texts of the Bible cannot exist without the revolutionary texts, and vice versa. These texts exist; they can't be cut out for a trimmed down, more palatable Bible. You can't choose the texts you like and forget the rest. This means that it is not merely an abusive and obnoxious text.

It follows then that the Bible may at times have emancipatory or liberating moments buried within its oppressive ones. We can't, however, simply leap into the Bible and find the liberating texts that suit us. Rather, only by keeping theological suspicion at the forefront can we use these texts as a wellspring of a viable struggle for freedom and justice. We don't want such readings of the Bible to be hijacked by theological pretensions, nor indeed by the robber barons of global capitalism. Thus texts that I will discuss in Chapters Five and Six, such as the legendary image of the early Church's communist societies in the book of Acts, or the call to 'Let my people go', or the stories of the Murmuring in the Wilderness when the people rebel against

Moses, must all be read with theological suspicion. While we recover the repressed stories of rebellion, we need to watch for their appropriation by Church and state. My point here is not a theological one, although it might be mistaken for that. It is a political one. Rather than some knee-jerk reaction that dismisses the Bible as a religious document, a sacred text, this point recognizes that the Bible may have a motivational power for liberation.

There are two reasons for such a search for emancipatory readings. Firstly, there is a long history in which the Bible has been used by groups working for a better society, for the alleviation of suffering and oppression. It is a history which I will trace in Chapter Five. Secondly, I think of a marvellous book by Michael Löwy called *War of the Gods* (1996). After considering liberation theology in Latin America, one of Löwy's most telling conclusions is that the old secular left needs to rethink its attitude to the Bible and theology, for sometimes they may well be on the same side.

A politics of alliance

Löwy's conclusion leads to the final element of the new secular approach to the Bible. Given that religious and secular readings of the Bible are inseparable at a deep level, given that the Bible has inspired revolutionary movements throughout its long history, and given that the religious and secular left often have the same political aims, it seems logical that they should develop a consistent politics of alliance. This means that the religious left is not stranded to fight its battles alone, surrounded by a rising tide of the religious right and all manner of fundamentalisms. It also means that the secular left may in fact find the Bible a source of political inspiration, as figures such as Ernst Bloch and Georges Sorel found.

Indeed, Sorel and Bloch, among others, show that I do not need to urge the old secular left to take an interest in the Bible, for there is already a history of such interest. Let me take a moment to say a little more about Sorel and Bloch. Georges Sorel (1847–1922) was a leader of the French left at the turn of the nineteenth and twentieth centuries. A heretical Marxist (the best sort), Sorel was fascinated with early Christianity and saw many affinities between Marxism and the early Christian movement. Rather than following the line of historical determinism – the famous 'history is on our side' position – that may be found in some types of Christianity and Marxism, Sorel was a strong believer in 'direct action', a phrase he coined. We should take history into our hands, he argued, as a voluntary and willed act, rather than sitting back and waiting for either God or the economy to do the job for us. As a Marxist and later anarcho-syndicalist, he argued for and was involved in boycotts, sabotage, strikes and the continual disruption of capitalism. Above all, however, Sorel is known for his idea that Marxism needs a foundational myth like Christianity. If Christianity has the myth of Christ's death and resurrection as its driving force, then Marxism needs the myth of the general strike. The truth of such a myth lies not in its content (he was not a Christian), but in its practical effects: the purpose of such a myth was to motivate the masses to bring about change, to generate solidarity and a revolutionary focus. On the need for positive myths for the left I think Sorel is absolutely correct, but Sorel is important here for another reason: the use of the Bible in order to provide insights for the secular left. Thus, along with his *Reflections on Violence* (*Réflexions sur la violence*, 1908), he also wrote *Contribution to a Secular Study of the Bible* (*Contribution à l'étude profane de la Bible*, 1889), returning to the Bible time and again in his later writings.

As for Ernst Bloch (1885–1977), as you'll see if you ever come across his official photograph, he did his best to look like a craggy and cranky prophet as well as write like one. The two great inspirations for Bloch's work as a Marxist philosopher were Goethe's *Faust* and the Bible. Not only does the Bible saturate his magisterial *Principle of Hope* (1995), but he wrote a book on the Bible, *Atheism in Christianity* (1972), which is really an introduction to the Bible for secular readers on the left. In his programme of a hermeneutics of utopia, Bloch found the Bible a great storehouse of utopian images and themes, which has provided the worldview and motivated generations of radicals to seek a better society. Bloch's favourite themes

30

are those of the Exodus and the rebellion of Korah against Moses (Numbers 16), and characters such as the Nazirites with their ideals of a simple communal life in obedience to the God of the poor, among whom he counts Samson, Samuel, Elijah, John the Baptist and Jesus. He loves Job's challenge to God – 'Here is my signature [on the indictment]! Let the almighty answer me!' (Job 31:35; see Bloch 1972: 110) – and the prophetic statements such as, 'Learn to do good; seek justice, correct oppression; defend the fatherless, plead for the widow' (Isaiah 1:17; see Bloch 1972: 110). Bloch eventually fell out of favour in East Germany – he was, refreshingly, too heretical – but he argued that it was crucial to understand why the Bible had been so power-ful in the revolutionary consciousness of the peasants who supported radical political change.

I will have more to say on a politics of alliance in the next chapter, but four points need to be made before I do. First, readers of the Bible need not be religious. The assumption that you need to believe in order to be interested in the Bible would have to be one of the strangest mak-ing the rounds today, and one shared by believers and non-believers. Yet we don't expect an art critic to be an artist, a literary critic to be a novelist or a poet, a student of classical Greece to be a believer in Apollo or Aphrodite, or a lecturer in French to be a French national. Why then, must a reader of the Bible have a religious commitment?

Second, the old antagonism between the left and religion, once seemingly set in cement, should be a thing of the past. We can well understand how those antagonisms came to be so. For instance, following the criticism of Christian socialism in *The Communist Manifesto* – as 'but the holy water with which the priest consecrates the heart-burnings of the aristocrat' (Marx and Engels 1967 [1848]: 108) – socialism and communism since the time of Marx became largely secular and often anti-religious movements. And popular opinion followed suit, so much so that if a Christian declared that she or he had become a socialist, then the assumption was that that person had lost their faith. It didn't help matters when the major churches also declared communism to be 'Godless'. But these are, or at least should be, things of the past.

Third, those who do believe are not necessarily reactionary or fundamentalist. The 200,000 members of the International League of Religious Socialists put the lie to that assumption. Both the secular and religious left have more in common that they might think.

Fourth, a politics of alliance recognizes the diversity and pluralism of the left. Rather than the long tradition of one small group on the left feeling as though it is the keeper of the grail, spending all its energy condemning other group as revisionists, deviationists or heretics, the sheer diversity of the left is one of its great achievements. Within this diversity a religious left has a legitimate and crucial role to play. I will not say more here, since this politics of alliance will be the subject of the next chapter.

Conclusion

In summary, the old programme of secularism has revealed a series of problems: intellectually, religion and the sacred can be held apart only with extreme effort; no matter how strong the separation of Church and state, religion has a knack of turning up in all manner of state functions; and secularization has not meant the disappearance of religion or religious authority. However, this critical perspective on secularism is not a sign of its demise, but rather of a new situation that may be called post-secularism. The other major feature of post-secularism is historical, for it marks the rise of a host of spiritualities and now religion itself on the public stage. Finally, I argued for a new secularism that has five features: the recognition of the entwinement of religion and secularism; the need for theological suspicion in reading the Bible; denouncing abuse of the Bible; supporting emancipatory uses; and the need for a politics of alliance. The new secularism may recognize the importance of this age and this world, but it also offers a sustained criticism of that world.

2

The Worldly Left: Towards a Politics of Alliance

Second Thesis: Since the religious left has been marginalized and has had the Bible stolen from it, and since the secular left is on the rise, in order to rescue the Bible we need a politics of alliance between the religious left and the old secular left. I call this alliance the 'worldly left', one that is as wise as serpents and as innocent as doves.

What, then, is to be done? – as Lenin asked, quoting Chernyshevsky, in a somewhat different situation. Here I pick up the last of my points in the previous chapter concerning a new secular approach to the Bible: a consistent politics of alliance between the religious left and (old) secular left, an alliance I call the 'worldly left'. Within such an alliance, a critically appreciated Bible can find a new role. Before I go any further, let me clarify my terms. By 'religious left' I mean those who struggle within the Synagogue and Church for justice and who find the Bible an inspiration for their struggles. They include both the reformers and the revolutionaries. It will come as no surprise that my preferences lie with the revolutionaries – the sundry Christian and Jewish socialists, communists and anarchists who we will meet again in Chapter Five. Yet for a politics of alliance the religious left also includes the reformers, those who prefer to tinker with the system in order to improve it in one way or another. This is where many of those who struggle for queer, gender, indigenous and environmental justice may be found. By '(old) secular left' I mean the various socialists, communists and anarchists who are deeply suspicious of religion of any stripe, let alone a crucial sacred text such as the Bible. They still follow the old model of secularism which they understand as anti-religious, indeed as atheistic. Such a position may have been fine in nineteenth-century politics, but it cuts off some extremely valuable allies and hobbles the programmes of the left. For now I will continue to use the two terms of religious left and (old) secular left – sometimes dropping the 'old' – but only as temporary placeholders until we can find a better term.

Apart from practical politics and questions of justice, the reason for an alliance between the religious and secular left comes out of my argument for a new secularism in the previous chapter. There I argued that secularism and religion, and thereby secularism and the Bible, are an inseparable pair. Now, many would regard this entwinement as an unholy embrace, or indeed a dirty little affair. Nothing could be further from the truth: the interweaving of secularism and religion is a major source of strength for both. Secularism would not be what it is without religion; nor would religion be what it is without secularism.

In this chapter, then, there are three steps in exploring the politics of alliance. To begin with, I sketch the way the religious left has been marginalized in Synagogue and Church. In their various struggles, the religious right has been able to claim the Bible for itself while the religious left has surrendered the Bible and the very definition of what it means to be Jewish and Christian into the right's hands. I follow this up with the need to rescue the Bible in the context of the resurgence of the left in general. This resurgence is a response to all manner of globalizations, all the way from Coca-Cola to terrorism, as well as the spread of the one-party state and totalitarian characteristics in countries that supposedly have parliamentary democracy. Then I sketch what a politics of alliance might look like, especially in terms of what I call a 'worldly left'.

Stealing the Bible: The Marginalization of the Religious Left

A cursory look at the religious landscape provides the following picture. Reactionary and fundamentalist, or so-called 'Bible-based', religion seems to triumph everywhere. In Rome, one right-wing pope is followed by another. The Roman Catholic hierarchy watches its educational wing closely in order to ensure a narrow orthodoxy among its teachers. On a range of moral issues, it rails against contraception, abortion and stem-cell research. It systematically weeds out its radical clergy and scholars. In the USA, Bible-brandishing fundamentalist Protestant Christianity is so deeply entrenched, especially in the southern states, that the primary question for teenagers is not 'Have you had sex yet?' but 'Have you accepted Jesus yet?' Climate change, peak oil, the disaster in Iraq, even the possibility of a Democrat victory in the US elections, are all signs of the imminent end of the world, the Rapture, Armageddon and then the return of Jesus (one may even find a 'Rapture Index' at www.raptureready.com/rap2. html, which is described as a 'prophetic speedometer of end-time activity'). In Australia, vast conglomerates, such as the Hillsong enterprise in northern Sydney, spread their mega-churches further and further afield. In verses such as 'A rich man's wealth is his strong city; the poverty of the poor is their ruin' (Proverbs 10:15) and 'The blessing of the Lord makes rich' (Proverbs 10:22), they tout a 'wealth gospel': God will bless you with wealth if you believe and are faithful, but will curse you with poverty if you are not faithful and sin just a little too much. Others, such as the Planetshakers in Melbourne, attract swathes of teens and 20-somethings to their mix of Christian rock and evangelical Christianity, urging young people to devote their lives to Jesus. In parts of the Roman Catholic Church of Australia where the conservative Cardinal George Pell holds sway, there is a systematic effort to return to a pre-Vatican II agenda, especially in theology, education and sexual morality, and Islam has become the great enemy. Even politicians are noticing, celebrating what they perceive

35

as the return to conservative religion and biblical values. In Iraq, the disastrous invasion of American, British, Australian and other troops has opened up battles between Sunni and Shi'ite Muslim groups. In Israel, conservative and Hasidic Jews continue to set the agenda on domestic policy areas such as immigration. In each case, the religious right bases itself on the Bible. In each case, they have driven the religious left underground. In each case, right-wing religious belief and practice by and large is wedded to right-wing politics.

It was not always so. Evangelical Christianity, for example, has not always been the religious soul of the political right. There was a time in the nineteenth century when evangelicals were the scourge of the establishment, when that establishment was the aristocracy and the established church. William Wilberforce (1759–1833) is perhaps the most noted example. Although he was a social reformer rather than a revolutionary, for Wilberforce evangelical Christianity meant basing his life on the Bible, and that meant taking on injustice wherever he saw it. An evangelical by the time he entered the British parliament in 1784, he saw a programme of social reform as a natural part of his faith. Texts such as Jesus's words in Matthew 25:35–6 were crucial for Wilberforce: 'I was hungry and you gave me food, I was thirsty and you gave me drink, I was a stranger and you welcomed me, I was naked and you clothed me, I was sick and you visited me, I was in prison and you came to me'. As was the famous Galatians 3:28, with its claim that 'in Christ' there is neither 'slave nor free'. Although he is most famous for his persistence in halting the slave trade (for 14 years he brought bills before the parliament before succeeding in 1891), he also vigorously campaigned to improve the condition of the working class, bringing in measures to counter inhuman working hours and atrocious living conditions, and he was one of the founders of the Royal Society for the Prevention of Cruelty to Animals (RSPCA). Now while we might find problematic his efforts to have the East India Company include missionary work in its charter, or indeed his personal motto – 'God Almighty has set before me two great objects, the suppression of the Slave Trade and the Reformation of Manners' – a little quaint, Wilberforce and other evangelicals like him saw their work of social reform, their challenge to the aristocrats of his own Tory Party, and their tireless efforts on behalf of the working class, as a natural extension of the Bible and their evangelical faith. Would that it were so now!

It is a long time since such a version of Christianity was seen to be consistent with the political left, no matter how mild Wilberforce may have been. What has happened since is that the religious right has become the provider of moral and biblical justification for the political right, and it uses the Bible in order to do so. If Jesus were alive today, goes the argument, then despite all its sins he would still vote for the right. He simply would not condone abortion, gay rights, indigenous land claims, efforts to deal with climate change, and the supposed atheistic stance of what passes for the 'left'. In the process *the religious right has stolen the Bible and claimed it as their sole possession.* A crucial move in this theft is the development of distinct language, or discourse.

Such a discourse is all too recognizable. Thus a church of the religious right is a 'Bible-based' church, implying that any other branch of Christianity is not 'Bible-based'. Further, being 'Bible-based' means that you focus on the central issues, namely your personal walk with Jesus. If you have accepted Jesus into your life – as the language goes – then you will want to learn more about him from God's word to us, the Bible, as well his gift to us, the Church. This Bible is of course inerrant, the inspired word of God ('All scripture is inspired by God' says 2 Timothy 3:16), and to question any detail, even the smallest, is to question God himself (the masculine pronouns are a signal of one's Bible-based faith). To take the Bible in this way, the only true way, is to accept that smallest detail, such as the sun standing still when Joshua asked God to do so in the battle with the Amorites:

> Then spoke Joshua to the Lord in the day when the Lord gave the Amorites over to the men of Israel: and he said in the sight of Israel, 'Sun, stand thou still in Gibeon, and thou Moon in the valley of Aijalon'. And the sun stood still, and the moon stayed, until the nation took vengeance on their enemies. Is this not written in the Book of Jashar? The sun stayed in the midst of heaven, and did not hasten to go down for about a whole day'. (Joshua 10:12–14)

The small matter of a geocentric universe assumed in such a passage may be overcome by the observation that God could of course do this if he really wanted.

Further, in this language of right-wing Christianity, your individual life of faith must be nurtured by a daily 'quiet time', when you read your Bible, with the help of one of the myriad guides so that you read it correctly, and pray. Social justice issues are just that, 'issues', and not central to the gospel. Sure, they are important, but too many people and churches get sidetracked by them. On some matters, the Bible is clear, such as the condemnation of gays and lesbians (Leviticus 18:22 and 20:13; Romans 1:26–7) and the subordination of women to men (1 Timothy 2:11–12), and we should not waste too much time on others, such as indigenous justice or environmental issues. Rather, what is really important is the spiritual battle between Satan and his evil spirits on the one side and God and the angels on the other. This is the vital conflict, and as a Bible-believing Christian you are a foot-soldier in God's army, overcoming evil wherever you might see it.

While this language may seem dominant across vast swathes of the Christian Church, especially those with a Protestant and charismatic background (and here I include those new churches that keep springing up like mushrooms after rain), it is a relatively new phenomenon. In the 1960s and 1970s, mainstream churches were largely liberal in theology and their understanding of the Bible. As a human document, through which you may hear God speak to you, the Bible was thankfully flawed and certainly not inerrant. It is, after all, a collection of documents written by human beings and they, as we all know, are somewhat fallible. You could sit loosely with many of its stories, such as the virgin birth of Jesus, or the myth of creation, or even the bodily resurrection of Jesus, and you preferred Jesus the Teacher rather than an almighty saviour. These liberal churches had small evangelical wings, but the evangelicals were definitely on the outer margins. However, as the mainstream churches began losing members for a variety of reasons, such as demographic change and the inroads of secularization, the evangelicals came up with a convenient narrative: these churches were losing members because they had lost their focus on the Bible and its central truths. They had become side-tracked on social issues, they had lost their sense of the importance of the Bible; they had become worldly and, in some cases, had lost their faith and the true way. Soon enough the equation turned up: Bible-believing churches grow, while those that are not Bible-believing decline. This belief slowly took hold, so much so that it is now dominant in many churches, despite the fact that statistics simply do not support it. Indeed, as Gary Bouma from Monash University points out (2006), the boom in the so-called mega-churches is not restricted to any particular standpoint, whether evangelical, charismatic, liberal or social justice. All the data points to the fact that the only defining feature of the mega-churches is that they are big, with memberships of 2,000 or more. They are well-run, offer a huge range of programmes for all ages and they are economically efficient. In short, it matters little whether they are so-called 'Bible-based' churches or not.

Despite these statistics, the picture painted of a rampant and all-conquering Bible-based Christianity is one that holds the imagination of the churches and of the public. In the process the religious right has stolen the Bible and claimed it as exclusively theirs. However, the response to this development has been contradictory. Firstly, the position has become so pervasive that many declining churches began 'evangelizing' programmes in order to halt the decline in members. They have of course had a spectacular lack of success in turning around the steady decline. By contrast, the second development is that the religious left has responded by focusing on identity politics – championing the causes of women's ordination, of indigenous rights, and gay and lesbian clergy, of environmental good practice, and so on. In each case, the Bible becomes the site of struggle, the focus of differing opinions and struggles, and texts are thrown at one's opponents with increasing ferocity.

However, let me make the following point here: the outcome of these struggles over identity politics is crucial for the future of the Bible in the Church; yet, conversely, the religious left has made a serious mistake in diverting its energy into such identity politics. On the one hand, it is vitally important that those who espouse justice on a range of fronts, from sexuality to indigenous politics, should gain the upper hand. The possibility of just societies depends on it. On the other hand, the move into identity politics as the key ground of struggle in these religious institutions is also a great problem. Why? The religious right has been able to designate these matters as 'issues' peripheral to the main message, if not waywardness from the straight and narrow path. Texts such as 'You shall not lie with a male as with a woman' (Leviticus 18:22) and 'I permit no woman to teach or to have authority over men' (1 Timothy 2:12) add ammunition to a religious right that takes the Bible as God's infallible word. In short, the religious right has been able to claim the Bible for itself while the religious left, as it takes on the various causes of identity politics, has surrendered the Bible and the very definition of what it means to be a 'believer' into the right's hands.

For this reason too the religious left has become a minority voice and is in desperate need of alliances with those outside Church and Synagogue. While I recognize the vital work done by the religious left within religious institutions, inspired as they are by the Bible, they are beleaguered and under attack from all angles by conservatives who seek to marginalize them in the name of orthodoxy. What the religious left needs, then, are alliances with progressive movements outside those religious institutions, with those individuals and movements who can assist in the long and difficult ideological and political battles, such as indigenous, lesbian and gay activists, feminists, environmentalists, and those who work tirelessly for equal distribution of resources, against hunger, poverty and exploitation. What such an alliance would show is that the various causes pursued by the religious left are actually parts of a deeper common political agenda.

The Resurgence of the Left

What we need to do then, is steal the Bible back, or rather, rescue it. And that rescue ought to take place in the context of a resurgence of the left in general. In this section my interest is the old secular left, in contrast to my concern with the religious left in the preceding section. We are indeed in a strange situation: as the religious left finds itself beleaguered on all sides, the secular left is in the early stages of a revival. This situation provides a distinct moment for rescuing the Bible from the political and religious right and reclaiming its revolutionary possibilities.

Before I say a little more about that resurgence, let me get two points out of the way. First, it is crucial that the old knee-jerk rejection of religion and its sacred texts by the secular left be dumped. Fitting perhaps for the nineteenth and early twentieth centuries, it is no longer a useful strategy. Second, lest there should be some suspicion that I am a closet advocate of religious institutions such as Synagogue and Church, let me be perfectly clear: I do not harbour any hope that they can become progressive institutions as a whole. You simply have to be kidding if you think they can on their own become prophetic bodies, offer possibilities of improving society or make the world a better place. They are inherently conservative, patriarchal, stuffy and often brutal institutions. Yet there are elements within them, elements I have called the religious left, that continue to struggle despite the odds, and their struggle is worth all the support it can get.

As far as the resurgence of the secular left is concerned, it would of course begin to take place precisely when old warhorses such as Terry Eagleton have been reciting the eulogy at the left's funeral, or at least the last rites on its deathbed (Eagleton 2003). Now, one may be forgiven for agreeing with him and others like him, for the rolling back of the communist bloc in Eastern Europe, the shift in China to rampant capitalism and the activities of rogue states such as North Korea have signalled for many the end of any viable socialism. On top of this, we have the great rush for globalization, in everything from military hardware to cultural kitsch, that has simply become a fact of life whether we like it or not. Without the need to compete with former communist countries, the welfare state slowly disappears beneath a vast reallocation of the state's resources. Even in bastions of the welfare state, such as in Scandinavia, the process of winding down is well under way, let alone in the USA, where one could well argue that even the glimmer of the welfare state has well and truly faded.

This is precisely the situation in which the left is able to get some grip. While some on the left may lapse into nostalgia for the good old days when there was something viable for which to hope and work (the ambiguous model of 'actually existing socialism'), they have missed the resurgence of the left in unexpected ways. What passes

41

under the name of 'terrorism' does not, of course, offer one of those ways, no matter how effective it may be on a mass psychological level. However, the context of 'terrorism' does. For what is happening in the rising hysteria over 'terrorism' is that parliamentary democracies are able to slip on the mantle of totalitarian regimes with remarkable ease.[1] In Australia a whole alternative legal system has been put in place that strips anyone caught in its net of even the basic elements of a fair trial. Detention without reason, severe penalties for reporting anyone so detained, and the withholding of all manner of information from any public scrutiny under the banner of 'national security' are just a few aspects of this system. One by one the critics of government policy are silenced and brought to heel, the latest being the two publicly owned media outlets, the Australian Broadcasting Commission (ABC) and the Special Broadcasting Service (SBS), who are under sustained attack by the government for 'leftie biases'. The same applies, with minor variations, in one state after another with parliamentary democracies.[2] At the same time, we live in what is effectively a one-party state. The major political parties – Labour, Tory, Liberal Democrat, National, Social Democrat, Republican or Democrat, or (fill in the blanks) – increasingly become factions within the one political party. So similar are the policies of these factions within the one party – the pro-capitalist party – that elections come down to popularity contests for the factional leaders.

We should not be all that surprised that the left – a proper left and not social democracy – should resurge precisely at this time. With a consistent history of the criticism of capitalism and the exploration of various alternatives, it does provide a clear option for those who see increasingly that the system is deeply flawed. It is, however, a left that looks somewhat different. All I need do is point to the return of anarchism as a version of radical politics for people in their teens and twenties; the common front of the anti-globalization movement, with its successes from Seattle to Melbourne; the varieties of green movements who continue to have a startling effect on popular consciousness; and the politicization of articulate and well-informed teenagers in a way that has not been seen for a long time. At a scholarly level, there is a renewed interest in the possibilities offered by Marxist, anarchist and post–colonial thought, not least among biblical scholars.

So the question remains, what on earth has the Bible got to do with all of this? Why would we want to reclaim and rescue the Bible in the context of a resurgence of the left? One answer is that with the profound shake-up of the left, the possibility of fresh and reinvigorating lines of thought and politics have opened up. Let me give a few examples, first from biblical studies itself and then from the secular left.

As far as the Bible is concerned, not that long ago Marxist biblical scholarship was an oxymoron, with one or two lone practitioners, but now it is possible to speak of a tradition of Marxist criticism of the Bible (see Boer 2007b). Marxism offers a distinct line of analysis that connects economics, politics, culture and history in the study of the Bible in its ancient context. I will give just two examples. First, in his groundbreaking work, Norman Gottwald has provided a road-map for the social and economic formations of ancient Israel (Gottwald 1999 [1979]). Adopted, debated, challenged and refined, his suggestion that we find a tension between a tributary and a communitarian mode of production has set the terms of discussion for the last 25 years. Second, Richard Horsley has been arguing for some time that we need to understand Jesus in the context of a militant and subversive Jewish peasantry in the face of a brutal Roman Empire. As a political criticism of the Roman Empire, Jesus enacted the kingdom of God for the sake of re-establishing a covenant community. Horsley makes extensive use of Marxist methods and archaeological materials to reconstruct the socio-economic situation in which Jesus lived and worked. He argues that although the Romans imposed a slave system in some provincial towns, the overall model in the countryside of Judea was one based on the old patterns of paying tribute to all manner of overlords, whether local potentate or more distant emperor. Under this system, a murderous tribute was exacted on the peasants (the purpose of the famed Roman roads). The peasants suffered a double blow, since on top of the Roman taxes the local rulers like the Herodian kings and Jerusalemite priests demanded their own taxes from the people while trying to flatter and imitate Rome. Resistance took the form of peasant slowdowns, sabotage, prophetic and messianic movements, scribal writings, counter-terrorism and revolts (Horsley 1989, 1992, 1995, 1996, 1997, 2002, 2003; Horsley and Hanson 1985).

As for the secular left's interest in theology and especially the Bible, there is a swell of reassessments. For instance, Michael Löwy argues in a study of the liberation theology movement (1996), especially its deep connection with the cause of the poor in Latin America, for a reconsideration of the role of religion within left thought and politics. The fact that certain elements of Christianity should be able to find not merely an affinity with the left, but a common cause from within its own tradition, including the Bible, is reason enough for such reconsideration. I would add to this that one of the deep sources for that tradition is of course the Bible.

Further, there is an intense interest in the Bible from a disparate group of left philosophers who are deeply indebted in their various ways to Marxism. Alain Badiou, with his roots in Maoism, has argued that in the writings of Paul in the New Testament we find one of the earliest and clearest expressions of the political event that breaks, entirely unexpected and undeserved, into the life of an ordinary individual (Badiou 2003b). Based on the fable of Christ's resurrection, Paul founds a militant political movement that is marked by faithfulness to that cause. The experience and expression of this event is for Badiou a truth, one that he also calls materialist or laicized 'grace', and is available to all. In response to Badiou, Giorgio Agamben has argued that Paul provides us with two crucial insights for a new politics of the left: the messianic and the remnant (Agamben 2005a). For Agamben, messianic time is the 'time that remains', a suspended moment (*kairos*) that grasps hold of a moment of our everyday, chronological time, and then opens up a possibility for it to be fulfilled in the future. As for the remnant, it is not merely the last survivors who somehow win through, but what happens when you keep dividing a group along different lines. For instance, when Paul starts dividing between Jews and Greeks, men and women, flesh and spirit, law and

44

grace, then you end up with an undefinable group that comes to stand in for the whole. There are others who have written recently on Paul, such as Slavoj Žižek, who finds that the revolutionary core of Christianity, embodied in the idea of 'Christian love' (*agape*), must be preserved at all costs (Žižek 2000, 2001, 2003). To Žižek's surprise, Julia Kristeva would agree, although she also argues that Paul's model of the Church (*ekklesia*) is an innovation that is able to soothe many of the social and individual pathologies that afflict us (Kristeva 1987: 139–50, 1991: 76–83). I could go on, citing Michael Hardt and Antonio Negri's evocation of a collective, political and very Christian love as the key to the multitude's construction of a new society (Hardt and Negri 2004: 351–2, 358), or Terry Eagleton's recovery of his days in the Catholic left, or Jacob Taubes's (2004) political reading of Paul's messianism from a Jewish perspective.

Now, one may agree or disagree with these various takes on Paul (I for one, much prefer Badiou over the others), or indeed other parts of the Bible, but that is not my point here. None of these critics from the left would count as a believer by any stretch of the imagination. And none would count themselves as a champion of the Church or of the Synagogue. Yet each finds in the Bible something for a reconstituted politics of the left. If you are at least a little aware of the revolutionary history of the Bible, which I will touch upon in Chapter Five, then all of this should come as no surprise. These critics are not the first secular readers to find the Bible politically relevant. There is indeed something in that curious but influential collection of texts that continues to inspire the left.

Towards a Politics of Alliance: The Worldly Left

So it seems that I do not need to urge the old secular left to take an interest in the Bible, for it is already happening. Indeed, there is more in common than at first seems between the religious and secular left. If the religious left, beleaguered as it is within the religious institutions, has access to a radical tradition of thought and action that precedes the

45

secular left, and if all the straws in the wind point to a resurgence of the secular left, then a renewed alliance may well be the way forward. Before I give a few examples of such an alliance, it is necessary to ask whether the old opposition of secular and religious lefts is a viable one any longer. I have called the secular left the 'old' secular left at some points, but that will no longer do. Is it possible to come up with a new term? Possibilities might include something like the post-secular or post-religious left, but we have too many 'posts' as it is – post-structuralism, post-modernism, post-colonialism, and so on.

Let me suggest instead the *worldly left*, a term that plays off both the religious and secular left against each other. To begin with, the idea of a worldly left returns to the definition of secularism that I outlined earlier: a way of thinking and living that draws its terms purely from this age and from this world. But 'worldly' also has a number of other connotations, such as experience, maturity and indeed worldly wisdom. To be secular in this sense means to be worldly wise. Now, there is a verse in the Bible that draws close to this sense of secularism. In Matthew 10:16 we find the admonition to 'be as wise as serpents and as innocent as doves'. In other words, the admonition is to be as worldly as possible, to have the wisdom and even cunning in order to know how to live in and of the world without, however, being caught up in its corruption and exploitation. Once again, wisdom, worldly wisdom, comes to the fore. At this point our definition of secularism and the text from Matthew come together, completing the proposal for a new secularism for which I argued in the first chapter. What we have, then, is a worldly wise, experienced and mature left, or, for the sake of brevity, a worldly left.

Further, the very idea of a politics of alliance, one where the various elements of the secular and religious lefts may work together, points to diversity of the left. The days of Marx's systematic condemnation in *The Communist Manifesto* of a whole range of groups, including the utopian socialists and the religious socialists of The League of the Just, are past.[3] It is no longer necessary – if ever it was – to seek out the revisionist, deviationist or heretic from our midst. Let me give one example: at the protests against the World Economic Forum in Melbourne in 2000 and

then again at the G20 meeting in 2006, we found anarchists, environmentalists, socialists, feminists, various elements of the loopy left, and
some religious groups for whom the protests were perfectly consistent
with the Bible. Further, the Marxist geographer David Harvey consistently includes some churches in his lists of those engaged in activism
against the ravages of capitalist exploitation, ranging from soup kitchens
for the unemployed and under-employed to protests and acts of solidarity with movements for political and economic change throughout
the world (Harvey 2000). A strange alliance? Not at all, for it marks
the presence of what I have called a worldly left.

Rather than proposing a constitution for such a worldly left, I
prefer to close with a couple of examples, one drawn from North
America and the other from South Africa. The first is Erin Runions,
who is both an activist and biblical scholar. Born in Canada, Runions
has been involved in various levels of activism with various groups,
first in Montreal, then New York and now Los Angeles. Working
with the assumption that all the energy and resources for war should
be redirected into food, Runions has worked with groups that gather
perfectly good food that would normally be dumped, prepare it and
give it to anyone who is hungry. Such a simple act has led to opposition by local governments and big business. She has also been involved
in anti-poverty, anti-war, pro-indigenous and pro-immigrant activities. However, for a long time Runions' activism was quite separate
from her biblical scholarship. Or at least it seemed to be separate.
With the beginning of the so-called 'war on terror', among others the US President, George W. Bush, began using biblical rhetoric
in his speeches against Muslim-majority states. The biblical claims
that God had chosen 'America' in a special covenant at this crucial
moment at the end of history were repeated *ad nauseam* in order to
justify a new era of global aggression. Before long, Runions found
her skills in demand in a different way, analysing and denouncing
the way the Bible is appropriated in neo-conservative thought and
practice as well as the speeches and justifications for war (Runions
2004a, 2004b). She even found herself reading parts of these studies
at anti-war rallies.

My second example is Gerald West in South Africa. Forced to flee his home due to political activities against the apartheid regime, West found himself in England and decided to study the Bible. Eventually completing a PhD at the University of Sheffield, he was able to return to South Africa to a teaching position. One result of his studies was the book, *Biblical Hermeneutics of Liberation: Modes of Reading the Bible in the South African Context* (West 1995), which has been very influential in South Africa and beyond. The two editions of the book (1991 and 1995) span the last years of apartheid and the election of Nelson Mandela as president in 1994. However, what interests me here are two features of West's work: his facilitation of the Institute for the Study of the Bible (which he has now passed over to others to run), and his comments concerning the role of the Bible in the Communist Party of South Africa. The Institute was initially modelled on a similar body in Brazil, called the Centro de Estudos Bíblicos. The agenda of the South African Institute is to 'establish an interface between biblical studies and ordinary readers of the Bible in the Church and community that will facilitate social transformation' (West 1995: 219). As with Ernst Bloch in a German context, the underlying awareness is that the Bible remains profoundly formative of the worldviews of ordinary South Africans. Some of the most fascinating work of the Institute is to read various biblical texts with different groups, such as the trade unions, Young Christian Workers and African Independent Churches. The parables of the Sower (Matthew 13:3–8) and the Mustard Seed (Matthew 13:31–2) produced some distinct interpretations. First, let me quote the parable:

> Another parable he put before them, saying, 'The kingdom of heaven is like a grain of mustard seed which a man took and sowed in his field; it is the smallest of all seeds, but when it has grown it is the greatest of shrubs and becomes a tree, so that the birds of the air come and make nests in its branches.   (Matthew 13:31–2)

Now for an interpretation from the Young Christian Workers, a militant group of young, mostly black, workers who seek to bring together their religious commitment and struggles for justice in the workplace:

To many, our actions might appear to be very small. This is like a mustard seed which a man took and sowed in his field. It is the smallest of all the seeds, but when it has grown it is the biggest of shrubs and becomes a tree so that the birds can come and shelter in its branches. What we learn from this parable is that even if our choices appear very small, through our commitment our small actions will give rise to big changes. This is the kind of commitment we have to take in the YCW.   (quoted in West 1995: 191)

This interpretation relates directly to the second aim of the Institute for Study of the Bible, namely social transformation. West has told me that for many members of the Communist Party of South Africa, which was a crucial ally of the African National Congress during the anti-apartheid struggle, the Bible was also an inspiration. At this point the crossover that I have been following and arguing for takes place: an old secular organization, nothing less than a communist party, draws from the Bible to carry on its programmes.

These are just two moments in what I want to call the worldly left, where the old divisions between a secular and religious left no longer apply. I leave it to readers to encounter others.

3

Bad Conscience: Battles Over the Bible

Third Thesis: Despite the best efforts to impose dominant view-points on the Bible, through canonization and interpretation, it remains an unruly and fractious collection of texts. For this reason it is a multi-valent collection, both folly to the rich and scandal to the poor.

In order to rescue the Bible, there is a prior question that needs to be asked: what kind of text is it that a worldly left may recover? Rather than a neutral text, it is a multi-vocal and ambivalent collection of texts, in terms of religion, politics, economics, sexuality and so on. In this chapter I show that we should expect nothing else from an unruly assortment of texts. In order to show *why* the Bible is multi-valent, I draw upon Ernst Bloch (the Bible is both folly to the rich and a scandal for the poor) and Antonio Gramsci (hegemony is inherently unstable). To show *how* it is multi-valent, I trace some of the key issues in the canonization and interpretation of the Bible. From there I move on to two case studies of a multi-valent Bible, one concerning Zion in Judaism and the other concerning the debates over identity politics in the Christian churches.

Before proceeding, a preliminary comment: because the Bible is multi-valent and unruly, it is impossible to insist that one interpreta-tion is correct and another not, that some misread the text and that others read it correctly. It is an old point, but well worth repeating: a whole variety of positions can be and indeed are justified by means of the Bible, whether political left or right, feminist or sexist, anti-racist or racist, inclusive or homophobic, and so on. Thus if one wishes to take a stand that is politically on the left – as I do – then some of the texts in the Bible and those who use them need to be condemned as abusers of people by means of the text.

A Multi-valent Text

There are two major, related reasons *why* the Bible is multi-valent: stories from the rich and powerful that condemn rebellion (as sinful and so on) actually preserve those elements they condemn; despite the efforts to tame the texts of the Bible and impose varying hegemonies on them, they remain an unmanageable and unruly collection.

As for the first point, I begin with a wonderful observation from Ernst Bloch, a leading Marxist philosopher of the twentieth century: 'The Bible has always been the Church's bad conscience' (Bloch 1972: 21). For all his faults and failings, Bloch's reading of the Bible in *Atheism in Christianity* is a model political reading. What does he mean by the statement that the Bible is the Church's bad conscience? Simply that the Church and Synagogue are in the end profoundly uncomfortable with, indeed somewhat embarrassed by, the Bible. It has an uncanny knack of undermining any position one might want to take. If the Church wishes to preserve Western culture against the perceived threat of Islam, then it must dispense with well-known biblical statements such as 'love your enemies' (Matthew 5:44), or, 'To him who strikes you on the cheek, offer the other also' (Luke 6:29), or indeed that Isaac and Ishmael are both sons of Abraham who played together when children (Genesis 21:9). If the church wishes to support a government that denies political asylum to those who seek it, then it will find texts that command one to 'love the foreigner' as God does (Deuteronomy 10:18–19), or the words of Jesus in Matthew 25:35, 'I was a stranger and you welcomed me', a little troublesome. On the other hand, if the church seeks to encourage peace, love and understanding, then the saying put in Jesus's mouth, 'I have not come to bring peace, but a sword' (Matthew 10:34), becomes problematic.

However, Bloch's reading of the Bible is both more political and subtle than it appears at first. He is not interested in playing the game of throwing proof texts at his opponents. That seems to be an approach preferred by those within religious institutions, for in digging up a proof text to back up one's position, you need to assume that the Bible is authoritative. And it is a well-known adage that for every position one can find another biblical text that contradicts it.

As for Bloch's explicitly *political* reading, he also points out that 'there is something very two-faced about it; something that is often a scandal to the poor and not always a folly to the rich' (Bloch 1972: 25). The Bible is claimed by institutions that are often powerful and wealthy, and that are often on good terms with powerful and wealthy rulers. I need only mention the Emperor Constantine, Charlemagne, Queen Victoria and Ronald Reagan in order to illustrate such an observation. Bloch does not have in his sights merely a string of venal popes, but even Luther – especially Luther – who sided with the powerful in suppressing the Peasants' Revolt of Thomas Müntzer in sixteenth-century Germany. Luther made very good use of the Bible to call down authority from above and to urge the faithful to focus on their inner walk with God. Indeed, if we go back beyond canonization (and the heavy hand of Constantine), Bloch finds that those responsible for gathering the stories in the Bible were the scribes, themselves part of a small and specialized elite in service both to the priests and kings. So one would expect that the stories they gathered would support the ruling ideology. For, as Marx pointed out, are not the ruling ideas those of the ruling class? So we find many, many stories of suppressed revolt, of insurrection brought to heel, beginning with the 'disobedience' of the first human beings in the Garden of Eden, running through the 'Murmuring Stories' in the wilderness to the call for repentance from one's sins in the New Testament. Of course, those responsible for such rebellion are cast as sinners against God and whatever ruler happens to be in favour.

So far, so good, but there is nothing particularly new in these observations. At this point Bloch's *subtlety* shows itself. It is precisely in these stories of suppressed revolt that we find the traces of insurrection. Bloch's point is that such traces have been preserved by means of – not despite – the ruling-class stories of control, order and suppression. For that we need to thank those stories. By representing the revolts in a negative light, by casting them as sinful rebellions against God or the gods, by outlining the punishments for those insurrections, the sundry priests, scribes, kings and emperors have unwittingly preserved currents of rebellion throughout the Bible.

A prime example of this preservation of subversive currents is in what may be called the Murmuring Stories, when the Israelites grumble and murmur against Moses, Aaron and God while wandering through the wilderness (Exodus 15:22–5; 16; 17:1–7; Numbers 14 and Deuteronomy 1:27; Numbers 16–17). One of the best moments comes just after the rebellion of Korah in Numbers 16–17. The revolt against Moses by Korah and his co-conspirators, Dathan, Abiram and On, is quickly and brutally crushed – Korah and company are swallowed up by the earth itself. But that is not the end of the story, for the people as a whole start grumbling about the way Korah et al. have been treated. In particular, the people murmur against Moses and Aaron for the act of suppressing Korah (Numbers 16:41 [Hebrew text 17:6][1]).[2] Moses and Aaron need some heavyweight support to deal with the revolt, so Yahweh steps in to assert Aaron's authority over those who murmur in discontent by means of a flowering and almond-producing rod (!). At this point we find the following key verse:

> And the Lord said to Moses: 'Put back the rod of Aaron before the testimony, to be kept as a sign for the *rebels* [literally, 'sons of rebellion'], that you may make an end of their murmurings against me, lest they die'. (Num. 17:10 [Hebrew text v. 25])

Note what happens: here Yahweh himself describes the *whole people* as rebels, or literally as 'sons of rebellion'. He speaks not of some subversive group or other that would still have room to move in a phone-box, nor even of Korah and company, for they have already been ingested by the earth a little earlier. As far as the text is concerned, describing the whole people as rebellious, as 'sons of rebellion', is a condemnation. And where possible, they get punished for that sort of rebellion. But that is Bloch's point: these deeply reactionary punishment legends and myths preserve the stories of rebels in the very act of casting those rebels in a negative light.

Another example of such a process of preserving a rebellious current while condemning it comes in the book of Esther. The story begins with a sumptuous feast thrown by King Ahasuerus for all his apparatchiks. After a massive binge lasting seven days, the king calls on his eunuchs 'to bring Queen Vashti before the king with her royal crown, in order to show the peoples and the princes her beauty; for she was fair to behold' (Esther 1:11). Not keen to be leered at by a bunch of drunken nobles, Vashti tells them to get lost. Her moment of rebellion draws a swift reprisal: the king's advisor, Memucan, recommends that she be deposed from her position and replaced by another woman. And what is the reason for such a punishment? According to Memucan, they must avoid Vashti setting an example for other women: 'For this deed of the queen will be made known to all women, causing them to look with contempt on their husbands, since they will say, "King Ahasuerus commanded Queen Vashti to be brought before him, and she did not come"' (Esther 1:17). The catch of course is that in the very telling, recording and preservation of the story, Vashti's rebellion itself is preserved. Condemned to be sure, but that is precisely how it is preserved.

This insight into the Bible provided Bloch with an explanation for something that had puzzled him: why did revolutionary movements time and again use the same Bible as their overlords for their inspiration to rise up against those rulers? His favourite is Thomas Müntzer and the Peasants' Revolt, which spread from sixteenth-century Germany to France, Italy and England, among whose descendants he includes the communist rebels in Eastern Europe after World War II. To those I would add Gerrard Winstanley and the Levellers in seventeenth-century England with their push for freedom of religion, suffrage and the abolition of kingship; the fight against slavery in the hands of William Wilberforce and fellows evangelicals in the nineteenth century; Martin

Luther King and the battle against segregation in the United States of America in the twentieth century; anti-colonial struggles the world over; the anti-apartheid struggle in South Africa; and most recently liberation and political theologies in Latin America and beyond. I will consider some of these in more detail in Chapter Five.

However, what all of this means is that the Bible is both a 'scandal to the poor' and 'folly to the rich' at one and the same time. But Bloch's point is that only through the stories that are a scandal to the poor – from the rebellion of Korah (Numbers 16) to 'Slaves, obey in everything those who are your earthly masters' (Colossians 3:22; see also Ephesians 6:5) – do those that are a folly to the rich survive. Or at least some of them, but it is enough in order to hear some muted voices. For this reason, according to Bloch, reactionary ruling authorities have used and continue to use the Bible to justify their policies and positions, while those who would overthrow those rulers also continue to use it to justify their acts.

Bloch's solution to this tension or ambivalence within the Bible is less than persuasive. He tries to resolve it by arguing that the reactionary support of power and authority that appears time and again in the Bible is a later overlay, something for which the late editors were responsible. Beneath these editorial layers we can find a truly revolutionary thread, in the oral stories and myths where the peasants threaten to do away with their overlords. However attractive such an argument may be, especially for the left, it falls into the old trap of finding some pristine origin, a core that has been corrupted by later overlays (it is a trap into which biblical scholars repeatedly fall as well). Rather than some pristine core, some original truth, it seems that we have a collection of texts that is thoroughly multi-valent all the way down.

This is where the idea of hegemony can provide some more depth to Bloch's argument. In a nutshell, hegemony means that any effort at domination and control is bound to be uncertain and shaky. In fact, the classic formulation of the theory of hegemony (a reworking of the Marxist theory of ideology), was an effort to find a way to overthrow those who oppress. And that formulation comes from Antonio Gramsci's notebooks, written while in Mussolini's prison (Gramsci 1992, 1996).

The point of raising hegemony here is that it applies so well to the Bible: despite the effort in the Bible to present a series of overlapping ruling and dominating perspectives, all the way from social organization to sexuality, not to mention religion, they are very shaky indeed. Or to put it even more forcefully (a point Derrida was to repeat after Gramsci), the very act of asserting dominance is inherently unstable. Subversion lurks in every murky doorway and under every bed.

Now, what I have presented as hegemony is not the popular view, or indeed the popular usage of the term. The popular concept of hegemony is that it is the dominant position, the one of the ruling classes. And it is reinforced by force (police, both secret and not so secret, law courts and army) and persuasion (propaganda in the media, education and argument). There is some limited truth in this perception. However, the problem with a ruling hegemony is that its position is inherently unstable. It is constantly undermined and must be asserted by as many means as are available and in whatever possible forum – such as culture, politics, religion and economics. These range from crude propaganda to subtle influence.

For instance, in the crude category would fall the regulation that all Australian schools must have a flagpole on which to fly the Australian flag, that it must be raised with due solemnity at a weekly assembly and the national anthem should be sung. An example of more subtle means would include funding behind the scenes for politically sympathetic groups and an ending of funding to government critics, or efforts to stress 'mateship', the 'glorious achievement' of Australia's history, or describing it as one of the world's great success stories (conveniently sidelining the brutal history of massacres of Aborigines and social engineering through the control of immigration).

Reasons for Instability: Canonization and Interpretation

In order to show *how* the Bible is multi-valent, I would like to give some examples – both crude and subtle – of the effort to assert control over the Bible. They come from the canonization and interpretation

of the Bible, for it turns out that both canonization and interpretation are failed efforts to control and colonize an unruly and fractious
mob of literature. Like any rowdy mob, it is not all that happy about
being dominated.

Brute force: crude assertions of hegemony

As far as canonization is concerned, Philip Davies's point hits home:
'The fact is that we do not know why a canon ... of religiously authoritative books was created, though we may reasonably assume that
its establishment was *a political act, intended to create consensus, counter
deviance and establish authority*' (Davies 1998: 182, emphasis added).
I have not italicized the last part of the quotation without reason,
for it is the key to understanding the canon. It means that unity and
consensus have been and continue to be imposed over a diverse, contradictory and conflictual collection of texts.[3]

Most efforts at making a canon (from the Greek, *kanon*, meaning
measure or rule) are crude attempts at hegemony. The blunt effort of
canonical inclusion is one such exercise of ideological power. It is a
little like the line-up for some badly paid job: you, you and you are
in, all for the privilege of a pittance, but you and you are not, so get
lost. Indeed, the process of canonization might be compared with the
way a dominant power deals with rebels (or, as they are conveniently
called in these times, terrorists?). The tried and true method is usually
a combination of 'divide and conquer' and 'if you can't crush them,
absorb them'. More specifically, we might identify three distinct but
overlapping strategies: division into rival and competing groups, exclusion and destruction of undesirables, and finally containment and
domestication of the remainder. So also with the various texts – and
the groups that championed them – that make up the Bible, where
we find a pattern of dividing difficult texts into rival groups, exclud-
ing and eliminating those texts that were too extreme (usually representing religious groups that lost the political battles), and co-opting
of the remainder.

Depending on whom you ask, the list of excluded books from the Hebrew Bible may number anywhere from the mid-30s to over 70, while for the New Testament the excluded books that survive number well over one hundred. Among the more colourful texts outside the Hebrew Bible we find the Apocalypse of Sedrach, the Syriac Apocalypse of Baruch, the Conflict of Adam and Eve with Satan, the History of the Rechabites, the Enochic Book of Giants, Eldad and Modad, and the Book of Jashar. At least they have survived, for many others have not. The issue at stake is not some inherently bad quality about these works (the usual justification from those in power), but that the groups that held these books dear lost the long and complex political battles for control. In some cases it is possible to reconstruct such groups, but in many cases it is no longer possible. That these texts survived is due either to the persistence or interest of such groups, a little good management and a lot of good luck, especially with the texts found in the Wadi Qumran.

The whole issue of inclusion and exclusion in the canon is very much a battle over hegemony. It would be too simple to argue that all of those excluded challenge that canonical hegemony, but some do. One case would have to be the Gnostics, and the Manichaean movement within Gnosticism. Gnosticism was a diverse movement, marked by a belief in a 'demiurge' or divine spark, correct knowledge, secret handshakes and whatnot. Manichaeism was a Persian variant of Gnosticism that looked to Mani (c. 216–76) as their founder with his radical dualisms of light and dark, good and evil, along with characters such as the Father of Greatness and the Original Man, and their radical sexual asceticism. Both groups found their texts rejected *en masse*. Both movements, albeit with all manner of variations and leaders and locations, produced a vast range of literature. Manichaean texts have turned up all the way from China to Upper Egypt. Apart from the seven texts attributed to Mani, all of which of which have been lost, there are 58 other Manichaean texts. These include a swathe of hymns and psalms, but also colourful texts such as 'Taste and Know that the Lord is Sweet', 'Come to Me, My Kinsman, the Light, My Guide', 'Parable about the Two Snakes' and the 'Psalms of Thomas'. Other Gnostics also produced a lively collection of texts, of which the finds at Nag Hammadi in 1944–5 provided by far the richest source. In this collection 50 Gnostic texts turned up, including the Gospel of Mary, the Gospel of Truth, the Gospel of Thomas and the Gospel of Peter. Other texts include the Letter to Rheginus, Treatise on the Three Natures, the Apocalypse of Adam, the Gospel of Matthias, the Gospel of Philip, the Acts of Peter and the Acts of Thomas. The Gnostics were prolific writers and included in their number charismatic leaders such as Marcion, Basilides and Valentinus. And yet, despite the range of texts and the popularity of Gnosticism among early Christians, most of the Gnostic texts were hunted down and eliminated. Apart, of course, from the Mandaeans, who continue in Iran and Iraq and have their own scriptures, the *Ginza Rba* and the *Haran Gawaitha*. The Gnostics and the Manichaean sect constitute a great reactionary front against which the early Church and then the state under Constantine had to defend themselves. So great was their challenge that they drew fire from some of the big guns from what became orthodox Christianity. So we find Irenaeus of Lyon, Tertullian, Origen, Hippolytus, Clement of Alexandria, Augustine (a convert from Manichaeism), Chrysostom, Jerome and Ephraim all bending over backwards to show how dangerous these people really were. They targeted Marcion, Valentinus or Celsus, or they drew in all the heresies they could possibly remember, along with a few extras that appeared in the odd dream or moment of paranoia.

Another example is one of my favourites, the Book of Jashar from the eighteenth century. One might quibble about the date, since 1751 (the date of publication) seems just a little too late for canonization. Yet if we consider the range of books within the canons of the different confessions, then canonization itself is an incomplete process. The Book of Jashar claims to have been written by Jashar the son of Caleb. It tells the story from creation to Jashar's own time with a few twists. For example, the tablets of the law were given to Moses on Mount Sinai not by God but by Jethro, the priest of Midian and Moses' father in law. The book also claims to be the lost book of Jashar mentioned in Joshua 10:13 and 2 Samuel 1:18, where certain events (the sun standing still in Joshua's battle with the Amalekites or David's lament over the death of Jonathan) is backed up by the words of a mythical book, 'Is this not written in the Book of Jashar?'. As for the daring forgery itself, it was, it says, 'translated into English by Flaccus Albinus Alcuinus, of Britain, Abbot of Canterbury, who went on a pilgrimage into the Holy Land and Persia, where he discovered this volume in the city of Gazna'. It was, of course, a glorious forgery and a challenge to the hegemony of Church and canon. Indeed, its publisher, Jacob Ilive, was sent to prison for three years in 1756 for publishing anti-religious pamphlets, including this particular act of forgery.[4]

For all its apparent stability, then, the canon is anything but stable, as the preceding examples show. Indeed, the plurality of canons is the most obvious signal of such instability, since no one hegemonic canon can in fact be established. All the way from the stark Protestants with their minimalist canon, through the Roman Catholic and Orthodox canons that have a whole group of 'deutero-canonical' texts such as Psalm 151 and the book of Daniel stories of Susanna and the elders and Bel and the Dragon, to the Oriental Orthodox canon that includes the book of Jubilees, what is precisely in and out of the canon remains an open question. It remains a fluid and unstable hegemony.

Gentle 'persuasion': subtle efforts at hegemony

So much for the crude efforts to assert hegemony over the Bible and its perpetual undermining. I also promised some examples of more subtle attempts at hegemony within the Bible. These attempts usually involve some level of gently doctoring the texts to suit the viewpoint of those in power – an observation here, an opening paragraph there – or an elaborate method of interpreting the texts so that they say what they are supposed to say. Indeed, this is where interpretation comes into its own, for it is generally a more subtle effort at persuasion.

An excellent example of editing a text here and there to bring it closer to the party line is the book of Qoheleth, or Ecclesiastes. One of three books in the canon of the Hebrew Bible that struggled to make the grade (the other two are the Song of Songs and Esther), only just making it in at the last moment, Ecclesiastes's problem is a less than pious nature. The opening claim, 'Vanity of vanities! All is vanity' (Eccl. 1:2), is not conducive to the value of religious teaching. Its well-known pessimism and scepticism – that life itself is a 'chasing after wind' (Eccl. 2:17) – run against the tenor of Torah piety. Indeed, one can detect what Mark Sneed calls an 'oblique criticism of God' in Ecclesiastes (Sneed 2004: 6). Thus, in 7:13 we find, 'Consider the work of God; who can make straight what he has made crooked?' Or 6:1–2:

> There is an evil that I have seen under the sun, and it lies heavy upon men: a man to whom God gives wealth, possessions, and honour, so that he lacks nothing of all that he desires, yet God does not give him power to enjoy them, but a stranger enjoys them. This is a vanity; it is a sore affliction.

And Ecclesiastes questions the notion of retribution that lay at the heart of the Wisdom movement and of Torah piety itself.

How does a piece of work like this become acceptable? Throw in a few editorial comments at the end, especially the closing verses: 'The end of the matter; all has been heard. Fear God, and keep his commandments; for this is the whole duty of man. For God will bring every deed into judgement, with every secret thing, whether good or evil' (Eccl. 12: 13–14). After all, the Preacher did write 'words of truth' (Eccl. 12:10). These comments read like nothing other than the final comments of the Department of (Canonical) Integration before it hands on its report. All it need do in addition is assert that Solomon is the author, now in his wise old age (Eccl. 1:12 is useful on this score: 'I the Preacher have been king over Israel in Jerusalem'), and the job is done. While the unknown authors of Ecclesiastes might turn in their graves at this act of integration, it is all rather gentle.

Another instance of editorial activity is the practice of attributing a work to a legendary 'author', preferably someone who carries some 'divinely given' authority. In fact the practice is rife throughout the Bible. So we find that Moses is 'author' of the Torah, David and Solomon of the Psalms, Solomon of Proverbs and the Song of Songs, Jesus of the parables and Paul of those epistles. Then there is the effort to patch together collections of sayings and attributing them to one or other 'prophet'. Isaiah is the most glaring example, but it can also be traced with Ezekiel, Jeremiah and the 12 minor prophets as well.

Paul is a particularly good example of this process, especially since there is a good chance that there are some genuine letters from Paul – a rare case of *ipsissima verba*. It would be difficult to over-emphasize the influence of the Pauline epistles, especially the Deutero-Paulines, or perhaps better the Pseudo-Paulines. The scholarly Paul – the one responsible for the seven letters of Romans, 1 and 2 Corinthians, 1 Thessalonians, Galatians, Philippians and Philemon – remains the Paul of a relatively small circle of New Testament critics, or rather that even smaller club of Pauline scholars. Far more influential is what we might call the Church's Paul, the one of all 13 letters, including the seven Pseudo-Paulines, especially the (in)famous pastoral epistles of 1 and 2 Timothy.[5] This is the Paul who so often comes through: stern and a little grumpy, his over-riding concern is for good order in the church and the avoidance of offence outside it. Any hint of some notion of grace that would provide the basis of a utopian community that breaks with the existing world order melts away before the need for discipline. So we find the regulations concerning women (1 Timothy 2:9–15), the 'house rules' on the correct behaviour for women and men, fathers and children, masters and slaves (Ephesians 5:21–6:9, Colossians 3:18–4:1; see also 1 Peter 2:18–25), the need to preserve the content of the 'faith' and 'sound doctrine' (1 Timothy 4:6, Titus 2:1–2), as well as the occasional piece of pop-medical advice such as taking a little wine for one's stomach's sake (1 Timothy 5:23). For all the debates over the meaning of the genuine Pauline letters, this 'Church's Paul' is the one that has had and continues to have the greatest influence.

As I mentioned earlier, the other mode of subtle co-optation is the process of interpretation, although as I will point out in a moment, it is also a battleground. One outstanding example of bringing all the ingenuity of interpretation to bear in establishing a dominant position is the effort to bring the Hebrew Bible into line with Christian theology. So interpreters in the early Church worked overtime to turn all manner of texts in the Hebrew Bible into predictions and anticipations of Jesus, and even of the Trinity. Let me give a few instances. First, the curse to the serpent in Genesis 3:15 becomes a prediction of the conflict between Jesus and Satan in the New Testament. It reads: 'I will put enmity between you and the woman, and between your seed and her seed; he shall bruise your head, and you shall bruise his heel'. Second, Isaiah 11:1–5 is co-opted as a prediction of Christ. The first verse reads, 'There shall come forth a shoot from the stump of Jesse, and a branch shall grow out of his roots'. Many other texts were pressed into similar service, such as Isaiah 53 and 61:1–4, and the New Testament works as hard as it can to bring such texts into line. The Gospel of Matthew would have to win some award in this respect, for it explicitly points out time and again that Jesus fulfils what was written. So we find texts like 'Out of Egypt I have called my son' (Matthew 2:15), which is drawn from Hosea 11:1 and becomes a prediction that Jesus would go to Egypt. Third, there are some real long shots, such as the interpretation of the three men who come to Abraham's tent in Genesis 18:2 as the three persons of the Trinity. After all, went the argument, if God went to meet Abraham, then why did he turn up in triplicate? As a final example, we see a continuous effort to appropriate the various major figures in the Hebrew Bible, such as Adam, Noah, Abraham, Moses and David, as 'types' of Christ – partial anticipations of key figure of the New Testament. What we have is a massive effort at the ideological appropriation of disparate and contradictory literature.

However, my own favourite in this whole process of gentle prodding and tugging to bring a text into line is the Song of Songs. A collection of poems that is all about the fecundity of nature, and the blend of human lust and love, it does not mention God at all, let alone offer any religious teaching. With its references to breasts, night sprinkles, hands in 'latches' or on 'bolts' (Song of Songs 4:5, 5:2, 4 and 5, 7:3), so much so that one can almost hear the slapping, squelching and groaning of sex, more than one question was raised about the Song's status as authoritative and canonical, especially in the first and second century CE (see Exum 2005: 70–1). In order to become acceptable, three factors played a role. The claim of Solomonic authorship was one (it is, on this level, a product of his virile and lusty youth), and the use of the Song in rituals, especially the Day of Atonement, is another. These two are already acts of ideological co-optation, but the most important one is the third – interpretation itself. Thus the Song's inescapable allegorical interpretation – that it really speaks about the relationship between Israel and God, or later for Christians about the Church's and God's love for one another – becomes not merely a crucial factor in its acceptance, but is also spurred on by that acceptance. Rabbi Aqiba's famous and oft-quoted statement, at least as it appears in the Mishnah, is a wonderful example of ideological appropriation:

> Heaven forbid! – No Israelite man ever disputed concerning Song of Songs that it imparts uncleanness to hands. For the entire age is not so worthy as the day on which the Song of Songs was given to Israel. For all the scriptures are holy, but the Song of Songs is holiest of all. And if they disputed, they disputed only concerning Qohelet. (Neusner 1988: 1127)

You really are one of us, Aqiba is saying, but you just didn't know it. This is not merely a classic case of the dominant or hegemonic voice speaking to a marginal one, nor is it merely an assertion of the Song's status within the canon. It protests too much, going overboard to make the Song fit in: not just holy, not a latecomer to the party who stands alone at the edges, the Song is in fact the 'holiest of all'. So much so, that, as far as Aqiba is concerned, there was no dispute over the Song.

However, interpretation of the Bible is a massively contested zone. For all the sophistication of interpretive work on the Bible, it is remarkable how shaky the control over the various texts that make up that collection really is. In the multiplying of endless sermons and in the careful discussions by commentators determined to find the answers to all the questions raised by biblical texts (along with many that are not), the battle over hegemony is waged with particular ferocity. Interpretation would have to be the most consistent and sophisticated approach for both asserting a dominant position and undermining it.

Let me return to the question of hegemony. Earlier I pointed out that hegemony is the shaky effort to impose ruling ideas over others. There is, however, a further feature of hegemony: it is continually undermined from within and without. A major reason that the dominant hegemony is unstable is that it must constantly deal with insurrection – in politics, social movements, ideas, personal beliefs and so on. In fact, the whole reason Antonio Gramsci developed the notion of hegemony was to find a way to overcome the dominance of the fascist state under Mussolini and capitalism more generally.

At this point I need to refine what I mean by the undermining of hegemony. There are in fact two types of such insurrection, one that might be called the palace coup, and the other the peasants' revolt. It is, if you like, the difference between revolution from above (chardonnay socialism) and from below (the peasants' and workers' revolution). The struggle over the dominant hegemony – a gospel of personal salvation or the social gospel, Luther versus Rome, or indeed Luther versus Calvin – is invariably the palace coup model. At this level, the struggle over hegemony is really one dominant hegemony versus another dominant hegemony, whether religious institution, political movement or new economic programme. One elite group ousts another elite group and the game stays the same. All manner of political, social and economic forces play a role in such conflicts, but they turn on the interpretation of the Bible. The Bible becomes, if you like, the focus of all these other currents. The conflict of interpretations becomes the site where social, economic and political differences are expressed.

The second type of interpretive undermining comes from below. Here we find all manner of groups for whom their interpretation of the Bible provides fuel for their revolutionary fires – the liberation theologians, religious socialists and communists, peasant rebellions, anti-slavery movements and so on. I will discuss these groups in more detail in Chapter Five, suffice to point out here that for these groups all those suppressed currents in the Bible jump out of the text and speak to them. However much it may have been edited and interpreted, there is still Job's challenge to God to answer for what has happened: 'Know then that God has put me in the wrong, and closed his net about me. Behold, I cry out, "Violence!" but I am not answered; I call aloud, but there is no justice' (Job 19:6–7). There is still the challenge to Moses and Aaron by Korah, 'Why then do you exalt yourselves above the assembly of the Lord?' (Numbers 16:3). There is still the call for the destruction of rulers and emperors (Daniel 2:36–45, Luke 1:51–3).

At this point, my discussion returns to my earlier comments that I drew from Antonio Gramsci and Ernst Bloch. The Bible is a multivalent text because the effort at hegemony over it is, in Gramsci's terms, an unstable one. Whether it is the crude form of exclusion or inclusion in the canon, or whether the more subtle forms of quiet editorial work or sophisticated interpretation, that hegemony is never certain and never completely attained. But it is also the case that, as Bloch pointed out, the very stories that seem to assert a dominant position preserve within them the seeds of insurrection. Thus, in Genesis we find stories about the suppression of rebellion, as with the primal one in the Garden of Eden, or of Cain's murder of his approved brother Abel. From Exodus to Deuteronomy we find a series of laws dealing with what can only be called an underworld – women, the sick and the lame, sexual 'deviants', witches and other sundry practitioners of the dark arts, even worshippers of other gods. Throughout the Pentateuch a cranky and recalcitrant people 'murmur' perpetually against the leadership of Moses and Aaron. These various myths seem to play with such rebellion, giving it airplay, before trying to show how crime, or rather, insurrection, doesn't pay.

Case Studies

Thus far I have dealt with the *why* and *how* of a multi-valent Bible. Now it is time for some case studies, one drawn from Judaism and the other from Christianity. However, one point must be kept in mind with the following case studies. It is common to distinguish between religious and cultural forms of Judaism and Christianity. The terms are vague, but 'religious' usually means that one is an observant Jew or Christian of whatever type, whereas 'cultural' indicates a much looser or 'nominal' attachment. You may have absorbed some elements of religion as a child, or it may give you an identity. If you work hard and perpetually delay relaxation until the job is done, you are supposed to be culturally Protestant, whereas if you gamble and party only to feel dreadfully guilty afterwards, you are supposed to be culturally Roman Catholic, and so on. While the distinction between cultural and religious Jews and Christians may be convenient, I am not sure that it is all that useful. The reason is twofold: both religious and cultural forms of Judaism and Christianity are shaped by the religious institutions in question, which may be designated by Synagogue and Church; the ideologies of these institutions depend on a collection of sacred texts. These texts give them a language and forum in which to air a whole range of issues and debates, including politics, economics and sexuality. So, while the tension over Zion may appear to be a question of cultural Judaism, it would not be so without the Bible. And while the struggles over identity politics in Christianity may seem to be more religious, again, those battles are unimaginable without the Bible.

Judaism: the tension over Zion

On a Friday evening in late July 2006, when the state of Israel was in the midst of yet another invasion of Lebanon, this time in a futile effort to root out and destroy Hizbollah, I was taking my youngest daughter to a guitar lesson with a boy on whom she was keen at the time. On the radio was an interview with a young Australian man of Jewish background who had decided to join the Israeli army. Before going to Israel he had given an interview with the radio station. It appeared on station JJJ, or triple j, as it is called. Once, in the 1970s and 1980s, triple j had a distinctly radical edge, and was the station of choice for the marginal crowds of teenagers and 20-somethings. Then it took a staid turn, its DJs aged and moved on, until in the early years of the new century it gained a new lease of life. It gave me a distinct feeling of *déjà vu* to find my youngest daughter turning to the radio station I had once preferred.

The reason this young man had been interviewed was that another Australian, Sergeant Asaf Namer, had been killed a few days earlier in Lebanon (Wednesday, 26 July 2006). Namer had been caught in an ambush by Hizbollah at the village of Bint Jbail (see Tadros and Pearlman 2006). Asaf Namer had come to Australia from Israel as a 12-year-old boy, completed his schooling and then returned to Israel to volunteer for military service in 2004. He was merely a month away from completing his military service when he was killed.

Like Asaf Namer, the young man who was interviewed on triple j radio had decided to enlist in the Israeli army. He was also an up and coming DJ, working at night clubs and aiming for a slot on radio. It was a sensitive and sensible interview, bringing the war in Lebanon home on a distinctly personal level for its mostly young audience. My daughter and I both listened closely.

The young man said that he had decided to enlist in the Israeli army – an option for him, but not so much for those who live in Israel – because he felt a sense of shame. When he was last in Israel, he said, all of the young men and women of his age were doing their obligatory military service. Yet here he was, a Jew who was not doing his bit for the state of Israel. So, after discussing it with friends and parents, he had enlisted. The interviewer asked him about his budding career as a DJ, and then asked if he thought about the political situation in the Middle East. What did he think about the moves to an independent Palestinian state, for instance? The young man became a little nervous at this point, saying that he did not get involved in politics or think too much about it. But then he went on to give a distinctly political answer: in the Middle East there are many Muslim states, he said, but only one Jewish state. He left his comment hanging, with the implication that the Palestinians should move and join one of the existing states, or that Israel should not come to an agreement that would lead to the establishment of yet another Muslim state (although an independent Palestine would be a mix of Christian, Jewish and Muslim Arabs). He did not say these things, however. What he did say was that whatever the state of Israel did, he would support it.

For all the varieties of Zionism, from socialist to revisionist, religious and Christian Zionism, the possibility of Zionism is unthinkable without the Hebrew Scriptures. Even the most cultural, secular or atheistic Zionist uses a term that appears time and again in the Bible. Originally the name of the hill on which Jerusalem was built, Zion appears mostly in the prophetic texts. Coming to embody God's dwelling place, the temple, city and then the people, Zion is the object of punishment and blessing by God, but also of return from exile. It appears most often in the Psalms and prophetic literature, and of those Isaiah has the lion's share. Perhaps one of the most influential is the ecstatic, utopian anthem from Isaiah, anticipating a future return. It closes with these words:

> And the ransomed of the Lord shall return,
>   and come to Zion with singing;
> everlasting joy shall be upon their heads;
>   they shall obtain joy and gladness,
>   and sorrow and sighing shall flee away.
>   (Isaiah 35:10; see also 51:11)

It is a sentiment, with or without the reference to God, that lies at the heart of Zionism. As does the following:

> The Lord will comfort Zion;
>   he will comfort all her waste places,
> and will make her wilderness like Eden,
>   her desert like the garden of the Lord;
> joy and gladness will be found in her,
>   thanksgiving and the voice of song.
>   (Isaiah 51:3)

The theme of Zion is, then, deeply biblical, and can be backed up by a good many texts. However, in its modern form, Zionism designates support for the state of Israel at all costs, and that is where a problem arises. For some, such as these young soldiers and a good many other Jews, the connection between a Jewish identity and the state of Israel is seamless. For others, that connection is a source of deep shame. Here the biblical texts concerning Zion are a real problem.

At about the same time as the interview on triple j radio, an opinion piece entitled 'Israel does not speak or act for every Jew' appeared in *The Sydney Morning Herald* newspaper (Benjamin 2006). Andrew Benjamin's credentials are rather different from the young DJ and the soldier who had lost his life. A practising Jew, although apparently for 'cultural' reasons, Benjamin argued that the state of Israel does not define what it means to be Jewish. Indeed, that is part of the problem – the seamless connection between the two. As long as Jews unquestioningly support the state of Israel, the pattern will continue of attacks on synagogues, Jewish cultural centres and Jewish synagogues around the world whenever Israel launches yet another attack on a neighbour. Benjamin's plea is that Jewish religion and culture should not be tied to a distinct geo-political entity called the state of Israel. Rather, that culture and religion should openly and robustly criticize that state whenever the need arises and not be dubbed anti-Semitic when it does. What does such a criticism look like? Judaism does not equal the state of Israel, nor does Judaism equal Zionism. Indeed, by 'hijacking the Holocaust' to justify the state of Israel, by linking Zionism and Judaism, the state of Israel sustains anti-Semitism. Thus there is no cultural or ethnic reason for supporting the state of Israel, nor is there a religious one.

Andrew Benjamin is by no means the only Jew who is aghast at the acts of the state of Israel and the Israeli army within and outside its own borders, most especially in the occupied territories of the Palestinian West Bank and the Gaza Strip. Nor is he the only Jew who finds the state of Israel and its justifying political myths – which usually go under that mixed bag called Zionism – problematic. Another is the Australian public intellectual, John Docker, who is a staunch anti-Zionist and critic of the state of Israel. Apart from arguing for a diasporic, cosmopolitan and non-Zionist identity for Jews (Docker

2001), in 2003 he and Ghassan Hage organized a cultural and intellectual boycott of Israel, signed by 90 intellectuals, in response to the continuing dispossession and brutalization of Palestinians (Docker and Hage 2003).

Hidden beneath this passionate and often heated debate is the Bible. Both the support of the state of Israel by the young soldier who died and the DJ who had decided to enlist with the Israeli army, and the opposition from Benjamin and Docker, have myriad biblical echoes. In order to bring out the biblical nature of this conflict, let me turn to some of the work of Daniel and Jonathan Boyarin, especially their 1995 essay, 'Diaspora: Generation and the Ground of Jewish Identity'. Their basic argument is that Zionism is by no means justified by means of the Bible: rather it is a betrayal of Jewish identity, which is necessarily diasporic. In taking this approach to Jewish identity they seek to break the connection between past suffering and current oppression: that past suffering is all too often used to justify current oppression and brutality. 'We suffered and survived in the past', goes the argument they oppose, 'so the present brutal means is necessary for our continued survival'. The state of Israel, of course, does not have a monopoly on such a narrative, but it is one that occurs in the story of the Exodus from Egypt and the occupation of the Promised Land of Canaan. I hardly need to point out that this story was and is evoked in the passage from the Shoah – the murder of six million Jews in the Nazi concentration camps – to the founding of the state of Israel in 1948.

This connection, between past suffering and subsequent oppression of others, is one the Boyarins seek to break. Let us see how these two founding figures of the 'new Jewish studies' do it. They draw upon two biblical motifs, which they call the Mosaic and the Davidic. While the Mosaic stresses the themes of wilderness, nomadism, exile and totalitarianism, the Davidic evokes ideas of settlement, cultivation and totalitarianism. The story of the Exodus from Egypt has both elements, both the wanderings in the wilderness with Moses as a somewhat direction-challenged leader, and then the invasion of Canaan, the slaughter and removal of the indigenous peoples and finally the founding of a monarchy on which King David's name is stamped for all time. The Boyarins seek to make a clean cut between the Mosaic and the Davidic, between Mosaic diaspora and Davidic totalitarianism. The first is a model for Jewish identity, while the latter should be dumped as quickly as possible (see especially Boyarin and Boyarin 1995: 328).

As far as the texts themselves are concerned, it is not for nothing that the most venerable part of the Hebrew Scriptures, the Torah, ends while the people of Israel are still in the wilderness. The book of Deuteronomy closes with the death of the incomparable leader and prophet, Moses, before he can enter the land. Moses lives, leads and dies in the wilderness, in diaspora, and it is this that the Boyarins find an extraordinarily valuable and biblical theme. The first five books of the Bible are not the only time such a theme appears, for in other texts we find that the time in the wilderness was much more desirable than the corruption, apostasy and abuse of power that came with a settled existence, a state and a government. Thus, for Nehemiah, while wandering in the wilderness the people 'lacked nothing; their clothes did not wear out and their feet did not swell' (Nehemiah 9:21). Only when they settled in the land did they throw away the law and succumb to corruption. For Jeremiah, the wilderness is a honeymoon period, a time of devotion to Yahweh, in which 'Israel was holy to the Lord, the first fruits of his harvest' (Jeremiah 2:3). It is, finally, that moment before the elaborate ritual of sacrifice, of burnt offerings, grain offerings and fatted animals that the text of Amos despises so much. 'I hate, I despise your feasts', says the Lord. 'I take no delight in your solemn assemblies... Did you bring to me sacrifices and offerings the forty years in the wilderness, O house of Israel?' (Amos 5:21, 25; see also Micah 6:6–7).

By contrast, the Davidic theme is one that focuses on a land, a state and a government, all based on the dispossession of another people, the Canaanites. Apart from the texts concerning Zion that I mentioned a little earlier, the key to this Davidic theme is the ideal image of King David, despite his many flaws, and above all the promise of an eternal line. So we find the statement placed in the mouth of the prophet Nathan concerning David's heir:

He shall build a house for my name, and I will establish the throne of his kingdom for ever. I will be his father, and he shall be my son. When he commits iniquity, I will chasten him with the rod of men; but my steadfast love will not depart from him … And your house and your kingdom shall be made sure for ever before me; your throne shall be established forever.   (2 Samuel 7:13–16; RSV, translation modified)

It hardly comes more unconditional and absolute that this. Indeed, these verses did a lot of service during the time of absolute monarchies and the divine right of kings in Europe. Here we have an eternal kingship, and a temple that is closely tied up with the king. Add to that a palace and city and the impression is one of the overwhelming permanence of the state. Once David becomes the key to hopes of some great restoration of the state (if it ever existed in the first place) in the prophets – see especially Zechariah 12:7–9 – then we can see how much the Davidic element is ingrained in the Bible.

The point is obvious but worth making: both Mosaic and Davidic elements are deeply biblical. The key for the Boyarins, then, is to favour one at the expense of the other. Jewish identity should, they argue, embrace diaspora, an identity that is not an identity: it is 'perpetually an unsettlement of the very notion of Jewish identity' (Boyarin and Boyarin 1995: 327). Of course, the Boyarins are staunchly anti-Zionist, challenging the claims to a mythical autochthony and indigenous connection to Palestine. Indeed, for them the biblical story is 'not one of autochthony but one of always already coming from somewhere else' (1995: 327). Only in this way can the entwinement of ethnicity and political hegemony be thoroughly undermined.

For all my sympathies with the argument of the Boyarins, it has at least two problems. The first is the challenge to indigenous claims to the land throughout the world. Their response to this problem is a little lame, for they distinguish between 'real' and 'mythical' claims to the land: real claims are held by native Americans, Australians, and Palestinians among others, on the basis of 'real, unmysterious political claims' (1995: 327). Mythical and unfounded claims, by contrast, are held by Jews to the state of Israel, and for that matter all other colonial occupiers.

The major problem, however, is that the Boyarins provide a brilliant example of the multi-valency of the Bible. Quite simply, in the very act of taking sides they throw into relief the fact that the Bible is a troubled and conflictual text. Folly to the Zionists it may be, but it is also a scandal for the anti-Zionists, for both the Mosaic and Davidic elements come from the Bible. Neither one is an imposition from outside the text. While the Boyarins may prefer the Mosaic element of diaspora as the (perpetually undermined) basis of Jewish identity, and while Andrew Benjamin argues that Jewish culture and religion needs to be severed from the state of Israel, our young DJ is also implicitly biblical and perfectly justified to base his claim to the Davidic element, should he wish to do so, on the Bible.

Identity politics in Christianity

As far as the Christian example is concerned, it would be no exaggeration to say that identity politics is the primary form of struggle within the Church in its myriad forms. The characteristic form of these debates is to argue incessantly over the interpretation of key passages of the Bible since it remains the authoritative text. Along with feminism, we also find the churches facing, adjusting and rejecting the claims of gay, lesbian and bisexual members; struggling over the claims of indigenous peoples in countries that began as colonies, such as Australia, Canada and New Zealand; beginning to debate environmental politics; and denouncing or supporting rising xenophobic policies relating to refugees and seekers of political asylum. At the risk of generalizing, let me gather the proponents of these various positions under the (very) loose banner of the religious left.

It is relatively easy to determine who is supporting what. For example, in the struggles over the ordination of women, the key text quoted by those supporting such ordination is Galatians 3:28: 'There is neither Jew nor Greek, there is neither slave nor free, there is neither male nor female; for you are all one in Christ Jesus.' Various key female figures in the Bible, especially leaders, become the new champions, such as Ruth, Sarah and Deborah in the Hebrew Bible, as well as Mary

Magdalene in the Gospels and Priscilla in the Pauline letters. Churches such as the Uniting Church of Australia, the Presbyterian and United Churches of Canada, most of the worldwide Anglican communion, the mainstream denominations in Britain (Anglican, Methodist, United Reformed, Baptist) and the Folkekirk in Denmark (Lutheran) and many others have established for some time now the practice of ordaining women to the ministry or priesthood.

Others have not. They hold dear texts such as 1 Timothy 2:11–13: 'Let a woman learn in silence with all submissiveness. I permit no woman to teach or to have authority over men; she is to keep silent. For Adam was formed first, then Eve.' These churches include the Roman Catholic and Orthodox Churches, and most of the conservative Protestant denominations, from the charismatic churches like the Assemblies of God to the Calvinist rump of the Presbyterian Church of Australia. In short, the mix of progressives and liberals support the leadership of women, the conservatives do not. There are, to be sure, some conservative churches that have progressive sections, such as the evangelical Sojourners group in the USA, and there is a persistent feminist movement in the Roman Catholic Church. But in the midst of aggressive moves from the religious right, these groups look decidedly forlorn.

In varying degrees you will find the religious left pushing for a range of other positions, and as I write the most contentious one appears to focus on sexuality. In the end, there are a limited number of options for gay or lesbian people within the Church. They may stay in the closet, which has been the traditional way to deal with one's sexuality and religious commitment. I was once a member of a church in which a significant number were gay or lesbian. However, the church in question had a long tradition whereby it was fine to be gay as long as you kept it quiet. The Roman Catholic Church follows a similar policy: while officially denouncing homosexuality and upholding the nuclear family, a good number of its clergy and members of religious orders are gay or lesbian. As long as it is kept quiet, there are no ripples. However, if one comes out, then there are two options left: leave the Church, which many gay and lesbian people have done and do; or stay in the Church and fight the battle to reconcile one's sexuality and religious commitment within a hostile and homophobic institution, all the while seeking to bring about a sea-change in long-held biases and justifications. This is the position I admire, I must admit, for it is an almost futile effort to reconcile very difficult realities.

However, the point I wish to make is that these battles hinge on the Bible and some crucial texts. Or, to be more precise, the Bible provides the language and reference point for conflicts that are overlaid with a host of concerns that are not merely sexual. Various social, political and moral issues can conveniently be aired through the Bible. Thus those who operate with the basic assumption that homosexuality is an evil that should be repressed, cured or rooted out, will resort to texts such as those in the purity codes of Leviticus that I mentioned in my discussion of the Christian right (Leviticus 18:22 and 20:13), as well as one or two of Paul's diatribes such as Romans 1:26–7: 'Their women exchanged natural relations for unnatural, and the men likewise gave up natural relations with women and were consumed with passion for one another, men committing shameless acts with men and receiving in their own persons the due penalty for their error.' Those, on the other hand, who wish to celebrate their sexuality draw upon other texts, such as the unmarried Jesus and his homosocial band of disciples as they appear in the stories of the Gospels, or Paul's wish in 1 Corinthians 7 that everyone should be as he is, unmarried and 'single', albeit afflicted with the 'thorn' in his flesh (2 Corinthians 12:7), or the story of the love of David and Jonathan (1 Samuel 18–2 Samuel 1) and Ruth and Naomi. Often derided as the mere slinging of proof texts back and forth between opponents, the very exercise of using proof texts in this way shows how multi-valent the Bible really is.

Let me use one more example – that of indigenous politics. This is of course an increasing concern in countries that were established as the result of European colonialism and where an indigenous population has both widely adopted Christianity *and* found a political voice. The two are, I have argued elsewhere (2001: 150–93), closely related. The vast majority of indigenous people in Australia are Christian and are either involved in indigenous churches or sections of the mainstream churches. Couple that reality with a series of crucial land rights decisions by the Federal and High Courts of Australia – Mabo in 1992, Wik in 1996, Yorta Yorta in 2002 and Noongar in 2006[6] – and the churches find themselves in the midst of questions about indigenous justice and land rights. Again we find the religious left by and large supporting the moves to land rights and the religious right opposing them, mostly in line with conservative approaches in state and federal politics.

In form, these debates are comparable with the hot issue of the nineteenth century, namely slavery. The abolition of the slave trade was led in England by the evangelical William Wilberforce, who used biblical texts to back up his position. It was also a central item in the debates of church councils in the USA, especially in the context of the US civil war. Texts such as those of the Mosaic laws forbidding the owning of fellow Hebrews as chattels (Exod. 21:2–6, Deut. 15:12–18; Lev. 25:39–54), as well as the ban on kidnapping (Exod. 21:16), were crucial texts used by abolitionists. They found themselves countering texts such as those of Philemon in which Paul sends the slave Onesimus back to his master Philemon, or the infamous 'slaves, obey your earthly masters' of Colossians 3:22–4:1 and Ephesians 6:5–9 (see also 1 Peter 2:18–25). All the twists, turns and splits over these texts may be traced in more detail elsewhere (Harrill 2006). But what is notable is the way the various strategies of the abolitionists – from ingenious efforts to read texts otherwise (*doulos* meant servant, not slave) to the search for a deeper immutable principle and the idea that in its time these texts were liberating – were to be repeated in later debates over homosexuality and the ordination of women.

With this brief view into the past, I would like to ask what the next battle of identity politics might be. Given the developments of the 'Earth Bible' project (www.webofcreation.org/Earthbible/earthbible.html) and eco-theology with their efforts to listen to the 'voice of earth' in the Bible – especially texts like that of Job – one wonders whether the inclusion of animals in the economy of salvation isn't on the horizon, or perhaps the ordination of animals to distinct ministries.[7] If it sounds just a little crazy, then so would the debates over women, homosexuality or indigenous rights have sounded in the nineteenth century.

Conclusion

The Bible, in whatever form it appears, is by no means a neutral text, for it is an ideological and political battleground. In light of its long history of formation and canonization, in which the battle has been over the ruling ideas that determined what should be included and how, it should come as no surprise that interpretation of the Bible has been and continues to be a battleground between various factions within and between the religions that claim the Bible. These struggles – over slavery, gender, political persuasions, sexuality, indigenous peoples, and so on – are a distinct feature of the Bible that will not disappear. How, then, are we to negotiate such struggles?

4

(Ab)using the Text: Conflicts in Politics and Science

Thesis Four: The Bible is too important and too multi-valent a text to be left to the religious right. Thus it is necessary to take sides with the liberatory side of the Bible, and in doing so we denounce the reactionary use and abuse of the Bible, for imperial conquest, oppression of all types, and the support of privilege and wealth.

Fence-sitting is a precarious business; done for too long, it can lead to an injury in some vital part. The Bible is indeed an ambivalent political document, both succour to the rich and powerful and inspiration for the poor and oppressed. But rather than throw our hands up in despair, now it is time to take sides, and I for one am going to side with the unruly and fractious text. This is of course a political decision, one that sides with a radical and revolutionary tradition in which the Bible has been a crucial player. Let me be perfectly clear about that political option: it is a decision that any political and economic programme that brutalizes people and nature is undesirable and should be condemned and overthrown. Anyone, any text, any position, that enables and justifies some groups to oppress others – whether such oppression is put in terms of economics, gender, race or ethnicity, sexuality, class, nationalism or species – should be overthrown with the passion of a 'good riddance'. This means that any text of the Bible, any interpretation, that is used for such purposes also needs to be condemned and dispensed with. One can of course take another position, but then one would need to show why such a position is desirable.

Thus in this chapter I focus on the way the Bible is used and abused for repressive political purposes and in the next chapter I recover some of the revolutionary and liberating readings of the Bible. In this chapter, then, my concern is the way the Bible is used oppressively in the domains of politics, science and education. Specifically, I criticize its use in constructing the political myth of a Christian Australia, in the continued efforts in the USA to insert that country into the Bible, and the way it is used in the debates over 'intelligent design' (the older 'creationism' or 'creation science') in education and science.

Two points are worth emphasizing before I proceed. First, I do not argue that these examples are always misinterpretations of the text. They do not always twist or reinterpret some deeper, true message of the Bible. Rather, the Bible has plenty of obnoxious and toxic texts that can be used quite easily as they are. When such direct *use* is done for oppressive and reactionary reasons, it is also *abuse*. For this reason, I speak of both the use *and* abuse of the Bible. Second, in criticizing the political abuses of the Bible in this chapter, my approach does not assume that the Bible is merely a neutral text that may be put to a political use or serve a political end. Or rather, the reason it may serve such political ends is because we find these political agendas – which may be designated as ones of oppression or liberation – within the multi-valent collection of texts that is the Bible.

Politics

Politically, the Bible is gunpowder on a geopolitical scale. Increasingly the machinery of the state seeks to enlist and is influenced by reactionary 'biblical' religion. In the United States fundamentalist Christians who assume erroneously that the Bible is inerrant have access to the corridors of power, and thereby a disproportionate influence on domestic and foreign policy. In Australia, they form a powerful lobby group in the inner circles of government, as well as an elected member of the Senate or Upper House under the banner of the 'Family First' party, touting the ridiculous agenda of 'biblical' and 'family' values. In Israel, ultra-conservative Jews generate the major tension in Israeli society between religious and secular Jews, controlling a restrictive domestic policy and pushing for a raft of measures that includes the dispossession of Palestinians.

In what follows, I examine two examples of how the Bible is used and abused in contemporary politics. One is drawn from Australia and the other from the USA. In both cases, the issue is the use of the Bible to remake a right-wing political myth. In Australia that myth seeks to make the *lingua franca* of politics distinctly Christian and right-wing, while in the USA the myth becomes a form of 'geo-piety' in which the United States seeks to step into the Bible.

Under the spell of angels: the vision of a Christian Australia

For Australia I am particularly interested in what is known as the Parliamentary Christian Fellowship, a group that includes more than a quarter (60–75) of the total 226 members of both houses (House of Representatives and Senate) of federal parliament. It is supposed to be bipartisan, with some Labor Party members, but it is mostly the preserve of conservatives in the Liberal[1] and National parties. I want to draw on the words of three of its members, namely Peter Costello, the long-standing Treasurer of the conservative government of John Howard; Tony Abbott, the loquacious Health Minister and reactionary Roman Catholic (a potent mix if ever there was one); and Kevin Rudd, the leader of the federal Labor Party.

As a preamble, let me begin with the decidedly uninspiring Prime Minister, John Howard, and his vision – if it can be called that – of Australia as 'relaxed and comfortable'. In this Australia dads go to work whenever their boss needs them, show 'mateship' to those who are just like them, wash the car and mow the lawn when they can, and go to church on Sunday (if they're not at work because their boss has called them in) with mum who has been taking care of the kids all week. In other words, his vision is one of Australia as one great heterosexual middle-class suburb, without those meddling Aborigines, ethnics, gays and greenies who can spoil your quiet evening walk with your dog.

This mundane 'vision', however, is not particularly Christian, nor indeed biblical. However, John Howard's hard-line Treasurer, Peter Costello, provides what we need. In Scots Church, Melbourne, on the National Day of Thanksgiving on 29 May 2004 Costello gave a speech. In that speech Costello peddled his own version of a Christian Australia – all by means of some blunt biblical exegesis. Let us look more closely at what he does with the Bible and then trace the implications. In his speech he engaged in some light exegesis, and all the texts come from the Hebrew Bible – Psalm 116:12, Exodus 20:1–17 and 1 Kings 19. The first is the text used by the Reverend Richard Johnson, in the first Christian sermon delivered in Australia, on 3 February 1788. It reads: 'What shall I render unto the Lord for all his benefits toward me?' No doubt the rapt audience of political prisoners, convicts and soldiers who loved being there took this verse deeply to heart, being profoundly thankful to God for all that he had provided for them in the long journey in the prison ships to this far corner of the world. The third text Costello cites is 1 Kings 19, with its story of the flight of Elijah from King Ahab. Elijah flees to sit under a juniper tree and asks to die. But God speaks to him in a 'still small voice'. In Costello's hands, the text becomes the basis of a small illustration concerning the need for faith and perseverance – just like Costello's – in the face of widespread spiritual and moral decay.

But it is the use of the Ten Commandments that is most intriguing, becoming for Costello the basis of '*our* law and *our* society' (Costello 2004, emphasis added). Here is Costello's interpretation:

The first Commandments: Thou shalt have no other God before me; Thou shalt not make any graven image; Thou shalt not take the name of the Lord in vain; Remember the Sabbath and keep it holy; are the foundation of monotheism.

The Commandments: Honour thy father and mother; Thou shalt not commit adultery; are the foundation of marriage and the family.

The Commandment: Thou shalt not to kill [sic]; is the basis for respect for life.

The Commandment: Thou shalt not steal; is the basis for property rights.

The Commandment: Thou shalt not bear false witness against thy neighbour; and Thou shalt not covet thy neighbour's property; is the basis of respect for others and their individual rights. (Costello 2004)

Whittled down to Costello's five commandments, what we have here are the foundation of monotheism, the basis of marriage and family, the respect for life, the respect for private property, and then respect for the individual rights of others. Or is that four? The ultra-slim version is as follows: 'And so we have the Rule of Law, respect for life, private property rights, respect of others – values that spring from the Judeo-Christian tradition' (Costello 2004). Moses, it seems, is responsible for the basic creed of capitalist society with its focus on the inviolable private individual. In fact, it seems that Moses would have been the first capitalist had he existed (and no reputable biblical scholar believes that he did).

Thankfully, for Costello, this heritage is distinctly Christian. All the same, it was a close shave, for Australia might well have been – God forbid – Muslim. I have discussed this matter in more detail elsewhere (Boer 2007b), but what I want to pick up here is Costello's comment on the origins of settlement of Australia: 'If the Arab traders that brought Islam to Indonesia had brought Islam to Australia and settled, or spread their faith, amongst the indigenous population our country today would be vastly different. Our laws, our institutions, our economy would all be vastly different' (Costello 2004). Thankfully for Costello this is not the case; instead Christianity came to Australia with the convict ships, bringing with them the 'single most decisive feature that determined the way it [Australia] developed', namely the 'Judeo-Christian-Western tradition' (Costello 2004).

'Judeo-Christian-Western' in Costello's mouth really means just 'Christian', as became clear a little earlier in 2004 when he asserted that Australia is based not on Judaeo-Christian values, but on 'Christian values' (Costello 2004, Hamilton 2004). What Costello really wants is a 'recovery of faith' (Costello 2004), or rather a recovery of *Christian* faith based on the Bible as the key to stopping the spiritual and moral decay of our society. And on this matter John Howard agrees: in his Christmas address of 2005, one that repeated a speech in Parliament the day before, he said that 'we do not deny our own beliefs as Christians, and the contribution of our beliefs to our values and those of our society' (Howard 2005).

As for Costello, his vision for Australia is a distinctly Christian one. Forget Muslims or Jews or those of any other religion in the faceless majority:

> They will get up tomorrow and go to their places of worship in suburbs and towns across the country, affirm the historic Christian faith, and go to work on Monday as law-abiding citizens who want their marriages to stay together, their children to grow up to be healthy and useful members of society, and their homes to be happy. They care deeply about our society and where it is going.
>
> These people will not get their names in the media. They will not be elected to anything. They will not be noisy lobbyists. But they are the steadying influence, the ballast, to our society when it shakes with moral turbulence. They give strength and stability and they embody the character and the traditions of our valuable heritage. It is their inner faith which gives them strength. Our society won't work without them.   (Costello 2004)

I hardly need to comment further on how this fills out the vision of a 'relaxed and comfortable' Australia touted by John Howard, except that now it is decidedly biblical and Christian.

There is nothing all that exciting about this vision. Bland it is, about as bland as Costello's futile efforts to take over the leadership from John Howard. We can, however, rely on Tony Abbott for a more exciting version of the vision, although it is excitement for all the wrong reasons. Perhaps sinister subplot is a better description. Abbott is a friend of the militantly reactionary and anti-Islamic Cardinal

George Pell of Sydney, and a member of the Lyons Forum, a large conservative Christian faction of the Liberal-National coalition government with an agenda of biblically based 'family values'.

So what is Abbott's vision of a right-wing Christian Australia? In his first speech as a member of parliament he quoted the same text as Peter Costello in the speech I discussed earlier – the text for the first sermon in Australia by the Reverend Richard Johnson on 3 February 1788. For Abbott, the words from Psalm 116:12 – 'What shall I render unto the Lord for all his benefits toward me?' – signal a 'message of faith and hope', one that is 'fundamental to our nation's success and the key to Australia's future' (Abbott 1994). More specifically, Abbott's vision is one in which Australia lives according to its Christian 'legacy', where the Church is 'the keeper of our culture's conscience' and source of its great art (Abbott 2007). Digging up an old anxiety from the nineteenth century, he asserts that the only basis for social morality is Christianity.[2] So far so good, but now we begin to glimpse the more sinister and ludicrous elements: Abbott's vision also includes thousands of pregnant teenage mothers and starving unemployed.

I joke not. To begin with, Abbott is beholden to conservative Catholic social policy, having made his job as Minister for Health synonymous with trying to curtail abortion in Australia, fighting a rearguard action against the so-called abortion pill, euthanasia, stem-cell research or therapeutic cloning (Abbott 2004), as well as awarding millions of taxpayer money to Roman Catholic family counselling organizations. To encourage elements of the Roman Catholic Church to be involved in abortion counselling is as about as intelligent as encouraging Osama bin Laden to organize scenic flights over Sydney.

Things get worse when Abbott resorts to his Bible. He often slips in a biblical reference or two into his speeches, such as the quotation from Paul in the context of a speech on unemployment and the work-for-the-dole programme: 'Disincentives to work have been recognised at least since the time of St Paul (who said that those who did not work should not eat)' (Abbott 1999). It takes little imagination to see what an employment programme that followed such a principle would look like. But Abbott goes on to use it to argue the old conservative position that those who are unemployed don't want to work and that therefore they must be given 'incentives' to do so, such as having their benefits cut or being made to engage in government-designated slave labour, euphemistically called 'work for the dole'. Yet in this case at least, the statement from Paul is torn from its context and given a loose interpretation indeed. It comes from 2 Thessalonians 3:10, from a letter not actually from Paul, but let me quote the whole section to give a sense of the passage:

> Now, we command you, brethren, in the name of our Lord Jesus Christ, that you keep away from any brother who is living in idleness and not in accord with the tradition that you received from us. For you yourselves know how you ought to imitate us; we were not idle when we were with you, we did not eat anyone's bread without paying, but with toil and labour we worked night and day, that we might not burden any of you. It was not because we have not that right, but to give you in our conduct an example to imitate. For even when we were with you, we gave you this command: If any one will not work, let him not eat.   (2 Thessalonians 3:6–10)

The problem for this anonymous author who pretends to be Paul is the right of travelling preachers in the early church to expect food and lodgings. This author sets himself above that example and wishes that others would not be a burden to those they visit. Of course, such a context matters little for Abbott. His gloss on Paul does reveal a central plank in the conservative agenda to roll back community support for those without wealth to back them up. Given his liking for such readings, we can well imagine the use of the instruction to slaves to obey their earthly masters (Colossians 3:22, Ephesians 6:5) as the basis of industrial relations policy – except of course that this verse may as well be the slogan of the new industrial relations policy of the liberal-conservative government that gives immense powers to employers and strips rights from workers.

It is a strange vision: a Christian Australia, full of backward medicine, pregnant teenagers, beggars, highway robbers and employees-as-slaves. Perhaps it is best summed up in a comment Abbott made after attending church: 'Under the spell of such music, angels can seem almost within reach' (Abbott 2007). Perhaps one can understand why the opponents of this high-profile health minister call him 'the mad monk'.

Initially one might think that the third member of the Parliamentary Christian Fellowship I want to discuss here gives us a decidedly different picture. Indeed, Kevin Rudd's ascendancy to the leadership of the opposition Labor Party has been greeted by many liberal and centrist Christians as a relief, as the proverbial breath of fresh air into the asphyxiating mix of religion and politics that has characterized Australian politics for the last few years. Rudd lays claim to be a social democrat – a term not heard in Australia for many a good year – who draws his inspiration from the Christian social gospel.

For example, he asks what government policy regarding refugees and asylum seekers might be if it took the story of the Good Samaritan to heart (Luke 10:29–37). It is just one instance of the biblical theme to care for the stranger in our midst, especially those who are vulnerable. Or how does the injunction from Genesis – 'have dominion over the fish of the sea, over the birds of the air, and over the cattle, and over all the earth, and over every creeping thing that creeps upon the earth' (Genesis 1:26) – influence matters such as climate change and environmental degradation. Should it not profoundly affect the local, national and international policies of an Australian government? Or what are the appropriate positions on global poverty, or the brutalization of workers under the industrial relations laws, or the focus on the individual at all costs in contrast to the collective and social?

These examples are drawn from an essay called 'Faith in Politics' that appeared in the journal, *The Monthly* (Rudd 2006a, see also Rudd 2006b). It soon becomes clear when reading the article that Rudd is far and away the intellectual superior of the likes of Costello, Abbott or John Howard. And he is far better read. In this essay, he identifies Dietrich Bonhoeffer as his hero. Bonhoeffer was the German Protestant theologian who found that the only Christian response was to oppose Hitler. And so he helped establish the Confessing Church, from which many leaders of the resistance came, spoke out on radio and in his publications, assisted Jews escaping Germany and then joined in with a plot to assassinate Hitler. Arrested in 1943 when the plot was uncovered, he was executed on 9 April 1945 at the prison camp at Flossenbürg, two weeks before the camp was liberated.

Rudd seeks to apply Bonhoeffer's criteria to Australia, especially those of speaking truth to power and speaking on behalf of those who cannot speak – the poor, future generations, the earth and so on. Now, as I mentioned, Rudd also identifies himself as a social democrat, just like Bonhoeffer, and toys with the phrase 'Christian socialism', pointing out that Andrew Fisher, the first majority Labor Prime Minister of Australia, was a Christian socialist. Here, at last, there seemed to be a coherent challenge to the religious right. Here is Rudd:

> I argue that a core, continuing principle shaping this engagement should be that Christianity, consistent with Bonhoeffer's critique in the '30s, must always take the side of the marginalised, the vulnerable and the oppressed. As noted above, this tradition is very much alive in the prophetic literature of the Old Testament. It is also very much alive in the recorded accounts of Jesus of Nazareth: his engagement with women, gentiles, tax collectors, prostitutes and the poor – all of whom, in the political and social environment of first-century Palestine, were fully paid-up members of the 'marginalised, the vulnerable and the oppressed'. Furthermore, parallel to this identification with those 'below' was Jesus' revulsion at what he described as the hypocrisy of the religious and political elites of his time, that is, those who were 'above'. (Rudd 2006a)

This may well be taken as rousing stuff, but when we look a little closer there are some disturbing trends. To begin with Rudd points out that he is not a socialist. Rather, he is very much in favour of capitalism. And he supports the principles of individual liberty, security and prosperity, just like his apparent opponents; all he wishes to do is add equity, community and sustainability. It is nothing more than capitalism with a compassionate face. Even more, he is a disciple of the 'robust, market-based tradition of Adam Smith' (Rudd 2006c), whose *Wealth of Nations* is nothing less than the capitalist Bible. For Smith, the environment, education and health are public goods needed for

88

a strong market. Unfortunately, this remains a conservative catch-cry, especially given Rudd's Roman Catholic background. Further, his claim that a Christian environmental agenda should follow the principle of being stewards of the earth is a loose interpretation indeed of Genesis 1:26. Rudd's effort to interpret this verse from Genesis in terms of 'stewardship' faces two problems: first, it is a soft translation for what should really be 'have control over' or 'have dominion over'; second, it is a very paternalistic view of environmental matters and places human beings in a superior position.

However, at deeper level there is something very conservative going on with Rudd's article and subsequent newspaper columns. He is, of course, seeking some traction against the alignment of the religious right and political right, and his is a call to Christians not enamoured with the religious right. The problem is that it *increasingly casts political debate in Australia in Christian terms.* The responses of Tony Abbott, Rudd's old sparring partner, show just how much this is the case. For Abbott challenges Rudd with other readings, but then says many of the same things. For example,

> It's hardly surprising that people who believe God became incarnate as a helpless child should have a particular respect for human life. Similarly, a religion whose founder proclaimed loving your neighbour was scarcely less important than a loving God [sic] has generated uniquely elaborate systems of social support. The faith-inspired basic ethical precept of Western civilisation, to 'treat all others as you would have them treat you', tempers the tribal instinct to 'look after your own'… Far more than any secular tract, the Gospels provide the foundation for the humane acceptance of difference that is the hallmark of our culture. Long before the term was coined, many Western societies were 'multicultural', under the (perhaps subconscious) influence of the parable of the Good Samaritan.   (Abbott 2007)

Abbott and Rudd, supposedly from different ends of the political spectrum, are starting to sound a lot like each other. Indeed, we can't avoid the conclusion that despite their apparent political differences (there are no economic differences at all), they both have a very similar vision of a distinctly Christian Australia. Abbott's vision may be a little more crazy and Rudd's may be a little more restrained, but then so is Peter Costello's or indeed John Howard's. All of the indicators – biblical terms of debate, the assertion of the Christian bases of social and political institutions, the mutual support of similar positions – suggest that at heart they are on the same side. It seems to me that we really do have a one-party state in Australia, for whom the terms of reference are now openly biblical and Christian. There is one pro-capitalist Christian party with different factions. Both support market capitalism, although they have different senses of how to make it work best. Both draw their basic terms from the Bible and the Christian tradition. Elections thus come down to popularity contests between the leaders of the different factions, which have the misleading names of 'Liberal' and 'Labor'.

What are the consequences of such a development? Let me conclude this discussion of abuse of the Bible in Australian politics with the words of another conservative ideologue, the Foreign Minister Alexander Downer. He laments what he sees as the Christian churches losing their way, and the most telling sign is the debate in the last 40 years concerning the resurrection of Christ, something he holds as a central tenet of Christianity, an absolute that cannot be gainsaid: 'the Christian church has always taught that belief in the resurrection was the central tenet of Christianity' (Downer 2003). But what does this mean for those religions that don't happen to believe in the resurrection of Jesus Christ? Downer offers this morsel: 'Of course it is possible to believe in God in some sense, or other, without believing in the resurrection, *as many good Jewish and Muslim Australians do*' (Downer 2003, emphasis added). Jews and Muslims make it in, but only as second class believer-citizens. One wonders what is left for those of any other religious faith.

Slipping the USA into the Bible

Although Australian politicians are becoming more forthright in their use of the Bible in political debate, the United States of America holds a huge lead in such practices. Ronald Reagan is only the most colour-ful tip of an immense iceberg, having infamously made the following observation to the then head of the American Israel Public Affairs Committee. It was later leaked to the Associated Press: 'You know, I turn back to your ancient prophets in the Old Testament and the signs foretelling Armageddon, and I find myself wondering if – if we're the generation that is going to see that come about. I don't know if you've noted any of these prophecies lately, but believe me, they certainly describe the times we're going through' (Wagner 2002:55).

Reagan is in fact one of a long tradition of 'theologians in chief' that may be traced back to Thomas Jefferson. A worthy successor in this type of apocalyptic rhetoric is Nancy Pelosi, former House Democrat Leader but now – since the 2006 mid-term elections – Speaker of the House of Representatives. The reader might expect me to focus on the far less worthy George W. Bush, especially since his use of biblical themes has been given much attention. He has enthusiastically set about appropriating the biblical themes of providence, the promise of land and prosperity, the apocalyptic moment (the way and hour 'of our choosing'), the sense of a militant historical mission and calling, ridding the world of evil and overcoming darkness with the forces of light (see Broadway 2001, Greene 2003, Runions 2004a, 2004b). George W. Bush's light is of course on the wane, and as I write the Democrats have gained control of both houses of the US parliament. The new Speaker of the House, and third in line for the presidency should Bush and Cheney both fall under a bus, is none other than Nancy Pelosi.

Indeed, Pelosi shows that Democrats are just as adept as Republicans in these matters. What Pelosi does is to locate the USA deep within the biblical text, ratcheting up to a new level the old and worn-out trope of the Exodus – in which North America is the Promised Land for the chosen people escaping the persecution of Europe. Here is Pelosi:

> As Israel continues to take risks for peace, she will have no friend more
> steadfast than the United States.

In the words of Isaiah, we will make ourselves to Israel 'as hiding places from the winds and shelters from the tempests; as rivers of water in dry places; as shadows of a great rock in a weary land.'

The United States will stand with Israel now and forever. Now and forever.   (Pelosi 2005)

The biblical reference is to Isaiah 32:2, but in the process of Pelosi using that text the USA slips *into the biblical text*. This desire is deeply ingrained in the US political myth, appearing in all manner of ways, such as the Mormon story of the lost tribe of Israel migrating to North America, or indeed the myth of the Pilgrim Fathers, or in a more secular form in the idea of 'manifest destiny'. For Pelosi, the USA becomes not merely the protector of modern Israel but also the protector of biblical Israel. We can sense her wish that the USA should have been there in the time of the Bible ('now and forever' goes backwards in time as well as forwards), for then ancient Israel would have been saved from imperial incursions. No Egypt or Babylon or Assyria or Persia or Rome would have touched Israel – nor will their modern successors.

This is not the first time Pelosi has caused the American Israel Public Affairs Committee to get all hot and bothered in apocalyptic expectation. In 2003 she told them:

More than a half-century later, our challenge is the same: how can America and Israel together walk the long thorny path and preserve Israel as a special place in the history of mankind? ...

... there are hundreds of college students here today. Allow me to speak directly to the students. Thankfully, you are too young to have witnessed the darkest chapters of the last century – the Nazism, communism, and authoritarianism. But in your eyes I see the glow of one of the brightest stars of the past century – the founding of the State of Israel.

You are the messengers to a future we will never know. It is your charge to build that future in the spirit of *tikkun olam*, the repairing of the world, in the spirit of peace and security.

On behalf of all who cherish freedom, thank you for your commitment to the ideals and values that define our two democracies – the United States and Israel.

My grandchildren tell me that this week begins the month of Nisan, the month of miracles, the month of deliverance. And over the coming weeks, Israelis and Jews everywhere will mark the miracles that have brought us to this day:

The survivors who endured the darkness of the *Shoah* and who braved their way to the light of Israel;

The heroes of Israeli independence who prevailed against overwhelming odds;

And all those who have defended Israel through decades of struggle and sacrifice, including a fallen hero Americans and Israelis mourned together – Space Shuttle *Columbia* astronaut Colonel Ilan Ramon, who literally took the Torah to the stars.

This is the spirit that defines the American–Israeli partnership. America stands with Israel now. America will stand with Israel forever.

We will never abandon Israel. We will never abandon Israel.

God bless you. God bless our men and women serving on the frontlines today. And God bless our special relationship between the United States of America and the State of Israel.   (Pelosi 2003)

Here we have one of the best instances of abuse of the Bible. Not only does the USA wish it was able to slip into the Bible, but it also has a vertical and horizontal relationship with the chosen people of the Hebrew Scriptures, Israel. On the horizontal or historical plane, Israel has a 'special place in the history of mankind', indeed, just like the USA. But that history is really mythical history, since the founding of the state of Israel and its future are actually moments in the mythical calendar. Thus the establishment of the state of Israel is linked with 'the month of Nisan, the month of miracles, the month of deliverance' and then we find the call to the young people to build a future in 'the spirit of *tikkun olam*, the repairing of the world'. Not content with the horizontal plane, Pelosi moves to the vertical: she has an Israeli astronaut take the Torah to the stars, except that the space shuttle *Columbia* exploded on the way back down. And then there is the basic mythical distinction between darkness and light: the darkness of the twentieth century, especially the *Shoah*, gives way before one of its brightest stars, Israel.

In light of the role of Exodus and Exile in the mythic narrative of US origins, we do not have to look too far to see Pelosi digging these up as well. So we find references to walking the 'long thorny path', a path that includes Nazism, communism, authoritarianism, and the *Shoah*. There are the heroes who prevailed against overwhelming odds, and since then 'all those who have defended Israel through decades of struggle and sacrifice'. Or as George W. Bush said, repeating the classic formulation: 'We're both founded by immigrants escaping religious persecution in other lands' (Bush 2004).

At this point let me quote Condoleezza Rice, the current Secretary of State, reinforcer of US imperial ambitions and globe-trotting myth-maker. For her the Exodus is at the forefront:

> In 1776, cynics and skeptics could not see an independent America, so they doubted that it could be so. They saw only 13 colonies that could never hang together and would surely hang separately. But there were others who had a vision, a vision of the United States as a free and great nation, a democracy, and one day, a complete multiethnic society. With perseverance, the American people made that vision a reality. In 1948, cynics and skeptics could not see *the promise of Israel*, so they doubted it, said it could never be fulfilled. They saw only a *wounded and wandering people* beset on all sides by hostile armies.
>
> But there were those who had another vision, a vision of a Jewish state that would *shelter its children*, defend its *sacred homeland*, turn its desert *soil* green and reaffirm the principles of freedom and democracy. With courage, the Israeli people made that vision a reality. (Applause.). (Rice 2005, my emphasis)

The Exodus is obvious here, with its 'wounded and wandering people' who are the Israelites in the wilderness, and then of course the image of the promised land that is both a shelter and sacred homeland. Further, the theme of 'the promise of Israel' finds echoes throughout Genesis and into the prophets. Among many examples, I quote two. Firstly, in Genesis 12:1–3 we find:

94

Now the Lord said to Abram, 'Go from your country and your kindred and your father's house to the land that I will show you. And I will make you a great nation, and I will bless you, and make your name great, so that you will be a blessing. I will bless those who bless you, and him who curses you I will curse; and by you all the families of the earth shall bless themselves'.

And then its echo in Isaiah 51:1–3:

> Hearken to me, you who pursue deliverance,
>   you who seek the Lord;
>   look to the rock from which you were hewn,
>   and to the quarry from which you were digged.
>   Look to Abraham your father and to Sarah who bore you;
>   for when he was but one I called him,
>   and I blessed him and made him many.
>   For the Lord will comfort Zion;
>   he will comfort all her waste places,
>   and will make her wilderness like Eden,
>   her desert like the garden of the Lord;
>   joy and gladness will be found in her,
>   thanksgiving and the voice of song.

Apart from these biblical allusions, I am very much interested in Rice's second paragraph that I quoted above, for it is far more ominous. In her 'vision' progeny and soil are lined up with that weary code for American values, namely freedom and democracy. But what happens is that sheltering the children, defending a sacred homeland and turning its soil for food begin to sound a lot like the reactionary myth of blood and soil that that was so beloved by the Nazis.

In both cases – an Australia in which the terms of political debate are increasingly biblical and Christian and a USA that steps into the Bible – we find the age-old efforts to claim a status of the Children of Light, or even the Chosen People, in order to valorize a distinct ideological and political agenda. Such moves are so hackneyed and unoriginal that one might be forgiven for wondering whether conservatives are simply unable to produce an original thought. Indeed, it seems as though there is no original bone in their collective body. The reactions from liberals and the left run all the way from cynicism to angry despair, with a good deal of hand-wringing in between. My point, however, is that it marks a wholesale and unabashed (ab)use of the Bible for distinctly political ends. It is, in short, a comprehensive effort at remaking a political myth, and a reactionary one at that.

All the same, we do need to remind ourselves that the Bible is an ambiguous political document. The likes of Howard, Costello, Abbott, Rudd, Bush, Pelosi and Rice do not so much abuse the Bible as pick up distinct strains within it that suit their own lethal political agenda. It seems to me that the scandal of what they do with this text is that such positions can indeed be found within and defended by means of the Bible itself.

(Un)intelligent Design, or The Battle over Malleable Minds

Alongside politics, the other great return of the Bible into the public sphere is in education, particularly the struggle between the theory of evolution and what is now dubbed 'intelligent design' – the argument that complex systems, especially biological ones, imply a designer. Of course, that designer is the Christian God and the model of such design is the story of creation in Genesis 1. A number of factors come together with 'intelligent design', especially the political programmes of the religious right, the battle over control of education, the culture generated around fundamentalist Christianity in which the conflict of our age is between God and his angels and the Devil and his demons, and the challenge to some aspects of the Enlightenment heritage, especially that of science. However, the pivot and focus for all these agendas is the Bible. Or rather, the Bible provides the language that fuels the political, educational and cultural programmes of proponents of intelligent design. Although 'intelligent design' is unthinkable without the Bible, although the Bible stands at the centre of the worldview in which 'intelligent design' is a major feature, the proponents of this position don't say this in as many words, at least not publicly. They are a slick bunch, especially when it comes to the heated battle to have 'intelligent design' taught in public school science classes. Their tactics, however, are not particularly new.

I remember some years ago receiving a telephone call, completely out of the blue, when I was for my sins listed on the staff of a church in Sydney. The advance party of intelligent designers had arrived in Australia and they had gone through the telephone directory, found 'churches' and systematically began calling the phone number of everyone who appeared in the list. With a zealot's voice, the man began by pointing to the underhand tactics of educationalists in corrupting the minds of the young with evolutionary theory. Feeling playful, I egged him on, and he launched into the anomalies and flaws of evolutionary theory, such as the three-legged dinosaur found in the same fossil bed as a poodle. How could anyone, he said, hold to such a theory when it was clearly flawed? Obviously they must have other reasons, such as the evil agendas of humanism, naturalism or secularism. It certainly couldn't be the cause of science, so the motivation of those purveying evolutionary theory must be anti-God. I asked what science really is, and he warmed up to expound the bullet-proof scientific credentials of 'intelligent design' – it is objective, scientific, and it could be held by Bible-believing Christians. The best thing was that you could present it to unbelievers and secularists without having to mention God once. It's just another way of packaging the Christian evangelical message, he said. God can just slip in the back door while we fool them. We call it the 'wedge strategy'. With my mind full of images of a vast cohort of Christian scientists with their underpants firmly jammed up their cleavages down below, I asked him what I needed to do. The least we can do, he said, was 'teach the controversy', show the public that there is a debate over evolution and creation and let people make their minds up. I wasn't sure that there was a controversy outside the heads of my good advocate and his close friends. More importantly, he went on, you should enlist in the battle for the soft hearts and malleable minds of the young. Under pressure, I declined, saying that I was hardly going to foist such gobbledygook on the savvy and street-smart kids under my care and direction. They'd laugh me out of town, I told him.

Creationism under a new name

Despite my best efforts, the 'intelligent design' movement has gained strength and regularly makes the news. A few facts never go amiss. At its basic level, the debate is between 'natural selection' and 'intelligent design'. The latter claims, in the words of William Dembski, that 'there are natural systems that cannot be adequately explained in terms of undirected natural forces and that exhibit features which in any other circumstance we would attribute to intelligence' (Dembski 2004: 27). It challenges the core assumption of evolutionary theory that chance, or 'natural selection', is the best way to explain the origin of life and its changes over history.

The theory of 'intelligent design' is by no means new, being a slick, tarted-up version of the older 'creation science'. The doddery 'creation science' based itself overtly on a face-value reading of the myth of creation in Genesis 1: God created the world in seven stages not that long ago, moving from light and darkness on the first day, through the creation of firmaments and waters, land and sea, vegetation, lights in the heavens, creatures on sea and land, and finally to human beings on the sixth day before taking a break on the seventh. All of this happened, claimed the creationists, in the order stipulated in Genesis 1, and not that long ago. The universe is quite young, because, they claim, the Bible says so.

At this basic level, 'intelligent design' is abuse of the Bible, especially Genesis 1, but also chapters 2–3. It begins with the assumption of inerrancy, one of the strangest ideas ever to be imposed on the Bible. Inerrancy supposedly means that in all matters of fact about the world, human life and the supernatural, what the Bible says must be held as factually 'true'. What it really means is that the worldviews or ideologies of the ancient Near East and then of the Hellenistic world, of which the Bible is one expression, are the worldviews we should adopt. Or rather, these worldviews should blend with each other: the assumptions of a capitalist system, in which the Enlightenment and scientific values of verifiable evidence and fact find their place, are imposed on the ancient Near Eastern and Hellenistic worldviews in order to produce the strangest of all mixes. So we find demons standing shoulder to shoulder with scientists, aeroplanes flying alongside God's flaming chariots, and earthquakes or tsunamis bearing the terrible burden of being God's punishments for our sins. As for Genesis 1–3, what is a creation myth or two becomes a factual account of how the world was created. I feel rather sorry for the Bible when it has to undergo such radical surgery, twisted and bent into all manner of shapes for which it is quite unsuitable. At this point, we should really let the book of Genesis get on with the business of being a collection of myths.

However, 'intelligent design' has quietly hidden its creationist roots before knocking on the doors of politicians and education planners, claiming to be hard science and seemingly at a distance from the Bible. Indeed, one might trace the pedigree of 'intelligent design' back to Thomas Aquinas's fifth proof for the existence of God in his *Summa Theologiae* (which employs the teleological argument), as well as William Paley's analogy of the watchmaker from his *Natural Theology* (1809). If one found a watch in the forest, goes Paley's argument, then one must postulate a watch-maker. The proponents of 'intelligent design' face an old problem, one that has been rehearsed time and again: it is a strange designer who would make the complex ingenuity of the AIDS virus, the wonders of a cancerous cell, or the prowess of flesh-eating bacteria such as necrotizing fasciitis.

In its recent reincarnation, 'intelligent design' as a term first appeared in the 1984 book *The Mystery of Life's Origin* (Thaxton, Bradley and Olsen 1984). However, the celebrated foundational text is the intriguingly entitled *Of Pandas and People* (Davis and Kenyon 1989), which is often put forward as an alternative science textbook by those seeking to include 'intelligent design' on school biology curricula. Following the trail of failed efforts to have the book introduced as a textbook by school boards across the USA is like following a caravan across the Bible Belt. A little detective work on the book reveals some amusing details. Although it is listed as published by Haughton Publishers from Dallas, Texas, no such press exists. Or rather, it is another name for Horticultural Printers from Mesquite, Texas. Now, one might at a stretch see the connection between creationist biology and agricultural publications, but printers are not usually presses. So it turns out that the publisher is in fact 'The Foundation for Thought and Ethics', a fundamentalist lobby group from yet another part of the lone star state (Richardson) that has been behind all those efforts to get the book into school science curricula. The fun does not stop here, for study of an early draft of *Of Pandas and People* shows that the text originally was sprinkled with 'creation' and 'creationist', only to be revised under the deft hand of Charles Thaxton, to 'intelligent design' and 'intelligent design proponent'.

Why the change? It seems that when the US Supreme Court in Edwards vs Aguillard (1987) ruled that the teaching of 'creationism' in public schools was unconstitutional – it was a religious theory that fell under the First Amendment's ban on advocating or establishing religion – the movement had to come up with another term to conceal its biblical basis. 'Intelligent design' was born soon afterwards. Its nerve centre is the 'Discovery Institute', especially its 'Centre for Science and Culture'. The explicit agenda of the Centre is to support 'research by scientists and other scholars challenging various aspects of neo-Darwinian theory', as well as 'research by scientists and other scholars developing the scientific theory known as intelligent design' (www.discovery.org/csc).

Positions

The ranks of the 'intelligent design' movement are not merely filled with quacks and scientific dabblers. A few seem to know what they are talking about, particularly when the key mathematical and scientific concepts are presented. One of these concepts is 'specified complexity', proposed by William Dembski, a mathematician (his claims to be a philosopher and theologian are on more shaky ground). The definition of 'specified complexity' is as follows: when an object is

both complex and specified, then we are able to postulate an intelligent cause. As Dembski puts it in his disarming style: 'A single letter of
the alphabet is specified without being complex. A long sentence of
random letters is complex without being specified. A Shakespearean
Sonnet is both complex and specified' (1999: 47). So also with living
things, argues Dembski.

Just in case one mathematical concept should be a little forlorn,
there is also a second, namely 'irreducible complexity'. This one is
defined as follows: 'A single system which is composed of several in-
teracting parts that contribute to the basic function, and where the
removal of any one of the parts causes the system to effectively cease
functioning' (Behe 1996: 9). The argument relies on an ingenious
sleight of hand. It assumes a building-block theory of development,
as though each part of a complex system was added one at a time,
much like a mousetrap, until it was complete, or indeed, much like
the narrative sequence of Genesis 1. Remove one of the parts, and the
whole thing ceases functioning. We might call this the 'analogy of the
mousetrap maker': God made the universe in a similar fashion to a
person making a mousetrap, piece by piece. Behe faced a small problem when he admitted, during questioning at the famous Kitzmiller
vs Dover Area School District trial of 2005, that all his examples, such
as the blood clotting cascade, the immune system, and the bacterial
flagellum of *E. coli*, were all explainable by evolutionary theory. Add
to that the fact that not one article arguing for 'intelligent design' has
been published in a peer-reviewed scientific journal, and we have a
problem.

Problems

What are we to make of all this? To begin with, the scandal of 'intelligent design' is that it puts on the airs and graces of being an 'objective' and 'scientific' theory, one that its proponents claim is equal to
or better than the theory of evolution (Meyer 2002). The affront to
the assumptions of science runs deep, as one sees by the condemnations from one scientist after another, among them the American

Association for the Advancement of Science with over 120,000 members (AAAS 2002), and a joint statement by 70,000 Australian scientists and school teachers (Archer 2005). The barb is that the proponents of 'intelligent design' acknowledge the canons of science, but then say that 'intelligent design' is science too. I can't help wondering whether the strong reaction from scientists and educators arises from deeper down: it is worth pointing out again that the various sciences too are based on particular myths, albeit different ones, and 'intelligent design' brings that truth a little too close to home.

Further, it is not for nothing that the conflict takes place in education. Thus we find a spate of efforts to have 'intelligent design' taught in one school after another in the USA. Not only are there efforts from 1990 to include *Of Pandas and People* in school curricula in states such as Alabama, Ohio, Idaho, Texas, Florida, West Virginia and Kansas, but the educational struggle is pock-marked by a series of court cases. From the 1968 decision of the Supreme Court of the United States, in Epperson vs Arkansas, the findings consistently uphold the First Amendment of the US Constitution: either they rule that a state cannot prohibit the teaching of evolution, or that creationism amounts to fostering religion in schools, or, most recently, that 'intelligent design' is not a scientific but a religious theory and therefore has no place in the schools. From the cases in Louisiana (Edwards vs Aguillard in 1987) to Pennsylvania (Kitzmiller vs Dover Area School District in 2005) the battle continues. Indeed, in the landmark ruling in the Dover case, the judge, John E. Jones III, ruled, 'we have addressed the seminal question of whether ID is science. We have concluded that it is not, and moreover that ID cannot uncouple itself from its creationist, and thus religious, antecedents' (Ruling, Kitzmiller v. Dover Area School District, Case No. 04cv2688, 20 December 2005). In other words, what the judge with the colourful name is saying is that the Bible is a religious book and not one that can be taken as an authority in matters of modern science.

One might point out that the whole debate is specific to the USA, with its strange mix of religion, patriotism and politics, along with the tension between some 90 million 'Bible-believing' Christians and the constitutional abhorrence of established religion that goes back to the founding myth of the flight from persecution by the established church in Europe. There is much to be said for this observation, as anyone who has spent some time in that strange area of the world called the Bible Belt in the southern states of the USA will attest. However, 'intelligent design' is the educational slogan of many conservative Christians in other parts of the world. In those countries, parents opt, where they can, to teach their children at home or send them to Christian schools where 'intelligent design' makes its way onto the curriculum.

All the same, it seems to me that the movement for 'intelligent design' has one major hurdle to overcome. All those who hold to the theory of 'intelligent design' are 'Bible-believing' Christians, and conservative ones at that. It would be a significant step forward for the proponents of the theory if a well-known scientist said: 'I'm an atheist, I think the Bible is rubbish *and* I think "intelligent design" is the best theory'. One suspects that this moment will be long coming, not least because saying it would involve being in a state of total inconsistency.

Conclusion

I leave it to the reader to explore other uses and abuses of the Bible in these reactionary ways – such as the justification of private property that goes back at least to John Locke (Locke 2003); the development of 'family values', in which the Bible somehow manages to justify the nuclear family; the oxymoron of business and financial ethics; the justification of hetero-normativity and homophobia, and so on. However, in regard to the abuse of the Bible in both politics and education, I am less interested in urging all those concerned to throw up our collective hands and cry, 'Omigod, isn't this terrible!' Rather, I am far more interested in the way the Bible is a major player in these ongoing battles. It does, however, have two slightly different functions. In regard to politics, we can see that the political multi-valency of the Bible itself opens up the possibility for the appropriations made by the likes of the Australian conservative cohort of Howard, Costello, Abbott, Downer and Rudd. By contrast, in the struggles over 'intelligent design', a different issue comes to the fore. It is not so much that the Bible itself is ambiguous, opening up the possibility of the ideological struggle going on in the multiple layers of education. Rather, in taking on education, the proponents of 'intelligent design' show that the language of the Bible is their language; indeed, their worldview is constructed out of the various raw materials provided by the Bible. That situation, it seems to me, will not disappear. In each case, however, and in others like it, a consistent and sustained effort of uncovering, debunking and denouncing such uses and abuses of the Bible is called for. It matters not whether the text comes straight from the Bible or whether it has been torn and twisted into some new shape. If they are used for politically reactionary purposes, then they are, quite simply, abuses of the Bible.

5

Making All Things New: The Revolutionary Legacy of the Bible

Thesis Five: Taking the side of liberation, we also need to recover the tradition of revolutionary readings of the Bible.

It is not enough to criticize and condemn the uses and abuses of the Bible for reactionary political purposes, although there is always a place – often quite enjoyable – for such activities. Taking sides in a multi-valent Bible and its various traditions also requires a positive appreciation of the Bible's revolutionary possibilities. Even if one is suspicious about such possibilities and would rather dispense with the Bible as a hopelessly reactionary text, it is difficult to get around the fact that the Bible has a long history of providing the motivation for revolutionary movements. That history, or at least select moments from that history, is the focus of this chapter.

Out of a long list of potential revolutionary candidates who have drawn on the Bible, let me dip into the dim and distant past to find Thomas Müntzer and the German Peasants' Revolt in the sixteenth century and Gerrard Winstanley and the Diggers from the seventeenth century. More recently there is the groundswell of liberation theologies, although I am most interested in the guerrilla priest, Camilo Torres. Müntzer, Winstanley and Torres are personal favourites of mine, but a little later I will have something to say concerning socialisms of the book and secular revolutionary movements that also found the Bible a source of revolutionary inspiration.

By revolutionary movements I do not mean Christian social thought, the social gospel or social justice movements within religious institutions, nor even those who draw on the Bible for the deeper doctrines of social democracy. However much I regard them as somewhat distant allies on a common front, I would like to invoke the old distinction between reform and revolution. What strikes a deep chord are not the various efforts at tinkering with the system, no matter how salutary those efforts might be (William Wilberforce's campaign in the British Parliament in the late eighteenth and early nineteenth century against slavery is one of the most momentous achievements), but those movements for whom the Bible provides the motivation for and language of utter change, a sweeping away of the old and constructing the new: in short, revolution.

Thomas Müntzer and the Peasants' Revolt

One of the most famous of biblical revolutionaries would have to be Thomas Müntzer, who operated for a few fiery years in the early sixteenth century. Let me begin with a snippet from one of his sermons:

> What a pretty spectacle we have before us now – all the eels and snakes coupling together immorally in one great heap! The priests and all the evil clerics are the snakes, as John, who baptised Jesus, called them, Matthew 3, and the secular lords and rulers are the eels, symbolised by the fishes in Leviticus 11 … O, my dear lords, what a fine sight it will be when the Lord whirls his rod of iron among the old pots, Psalm 2.   (Müntzer 1988: 244–5)

The key text was Daniel 2, around which the sermon weaves, although Müntzer peppers his sermon with many other biblical references. Indeed, his writings continually weave biblical phrases in with references to texts, as the quotation above shows all too well. Daniel 2 tells the story of the dream of King Nebuchadnezzar of Babylon in which he saw a huge image with the proverbial feet of clay. Its head 'was of fine gold, its breast and arms of silver, its belly and thighs of bronze, its legs of iron, its feet partly of iron and partly of clay' (Daniel 2:32–3). A stone smashed the feet of the image and the rest of it also crumbles, while the stone 'became a great mountain and filled the whole earth' (Daniel 2:35). Daniel is able not merely to provide an interpretation, but to tell the king the content of his dream as well. And that interpretation is that the various parts of the statue represent different kingdoms: Nebuchadnezzar's is the one of gold, but after him will come kingdoms of silver and bronze, and then the one of iron. However, since it is mixed with clay, the kingdom of iron will be a divided kingdom, 'partly strong and partly brittle' (Daniel 2:42) until an almighty kingdom established by God, represented by the stone, will 'break in pieces all these kingdoms and bring them to an end' (Daniel 2:44).

As far as Müntzer was concerned, the message was clear: God is bringing in a heavenly kingdom which will crush all corrupt earthly kingdoms. The audience comprised the two princes of Saxony, and the sermon was delivered in Allstedt on 13 July 1524. Müntzer went on to proclaim: 'He to whom all power is given in heaven and on earth is taking the government into his own hands' (Müntzer 1988: 251–2). The princes, however, did not heed his call to become part of the heavenly kingdom of Daniel 2 and to 'seize the very roots of government, following the command of Christ' (Müntzer 1988: 247), so he took things into his own hands, only to come to a grisly end after the fateful battle of Frankenhausen on 15 May 1525. Eight thousand peasants had lined up with him and they expected God to intervene and make their hoes and pitchforks invincible. They were to become the army of the kingdom that 'shall stand forever' (Daniel 2:44). Unfortunately, as is the way of these things, the heavy artillery and trained foot soldiers of the princes prevailed and the peasants were thoroughly routed. Müntzer lost his head on 27 May in Mühlhausen in Thuringia and his head and body were put on display as a warning to all such revolutionaries.

But what is it about Müntzer that makes him a biblical revolutionary? For some he was a religious crackpot, while for others he was the first spark of the radical edge of the Reformation, and for others still he was one of the many paths that the ferment of those years might take. There is, however, a distinct feature of Müntzer that marks him off from many of the others: he saw the resistance to oppression as the heart of the biblical message. That message was not merely some add-on, a political and social cause for which he found the Bible useful. Rather, the Bible itself mandated that he must, in obedience to God, denounce and overthrow the powers that oppress both spiritually and materially. In other words, the eternal kingdom of God was a revolutionary one, and he was called to be a leader in that revolution.

Martin Luther, the one who had stood up to the powers of Rome in the name of the Bible, found this unacceptable. Müntzer was in fact a contemporary of Luther, not living past his mid-thirties (c. 1489 to 27 May 1525) before his grisly end. His early life was reasonably conventional: born in the village of Stolberg in the Thuringia region of what became central Germany, he took his MA degree in biblical studies on his way to the priesthood, to which he was ordained in 1513. However, his stay in Wittenberg between 1517 and 1519, where he met Luther and heard his denunciations of the Church, turned his life around. The criticisms of priestly graft and venality struck a deep chord.

The catch was that Müntzer took these criticisms further than Luther was prepared to go – the revolutionary Müntzer showed how much of a reformer Luther really was, and a conservative one at that. From here on Müntzer was on a path of increasingly radical readings of the Bible. For Luther, who had initially recommended that he take up the parish of Zwickau in 1520, it was a sign of straying further and further from the true path. For Müntzer, of course, it was a gradual path to the truth itself. Well, not all that gradual: within a year he was on the road again, having been expelled from Zwickau. In Prague, his next port of call, he lasted only six months and was out by Christmas of 1521. Indeed, by the time of the apocalyptic and revolutionary work known as the *Prague Manifesto* (Müntzer 1988: 357–79), which he wrote towards the end of his time there, his initial enthusiasm for Luther's reforms must have seemed lukewarm at best.

Here he is again, in the *Prague Manifesto*:

O ho, how ripe the rotten apples are! O ho, how rotten the elect have become! The time of harvest has come! That is why he himself has hired me for his harvest. I have sharpened my sickle [Joel 3:13; Revelation 14:14–20], for my thoughts yearn for the truth and with my lips, skin, hands, hair, soul, body and life I call down curses on unbelievers … Help me for the sake of the blood of Christ to fight against these high enemies of the faith. I will confound them before your very eyes in the spirit of Elijah. For the new apostolic church will start in your land and then spread everywhere. (Müntzer 1988: 371)

From then on Müntzer became what would later be called a professional revolutionary, on the run, challenging the authorities, finding a safe haven for a time where he would attempt yet another coup. In Allstedt, a town in his home area of Thuringia, he became the pastor and fomented unrest for little over a year before he had to flee again in the middle of 1525. The man was no intellectual slouch, managing to produce in the midst of everything voluminous correspondence; a highly creative and original liturgy, the first in German; texts such as *Counterfeit Faith* and *Protestation or Proposition*, among many others (see the collection in Müntzer 1988).

By now Luther had had enough. After Müntzer refused to meet with him privately, Luther attacked him in his *Letter to the Princes* (July 1524), a direct response to Müntzer's *Sermon to the Princes*. Müntzer replied with his *Vindication and Refutation* (Müntzer 1988: 327–50), and let Luther have it, invoking one biblical text after another and calling him a wily black crow, a boasting, venal and wily fox, and 'Doctor Liar'. Luther also urged Duke John of Saxony to take action, so the Duke closed the printing press in Allstedt and called Müntzer to a hearing. Müntzer was a rebel on the run, attempting a coup in Mühlhausen mid-1524 that at first failed, and then succeeded for a few months in early 1525. This was the famous 'Eternal League of God', established by popular election from the citizens of the city, based on God's justice, the removal of those with power and wealth and the exercise of justice by and for the poor, outlined in the revolutionary *Mühlhausen Articles* (Müntzer 1988: 455–9). 'In this whole matter', he wrote, 'we want action taken without vacillation, without any delay, and in accordance with the word of God' (Müntzer 1988: 458). Soon afterwards, Müntzer would lead his ragtag peasant army to meet their maker at the battle of Frankenhausen.

What are we to make of Müntzer? Religious crackpot, reformer gone off the rails, apocalyptic plotter, hopeless dreamer, or impractical prophet? Is not history full of such figures, concerning whom we can only shake our heads and wonder? Except, of course, for those who do succeed, and then they become heroes in hindsight. There are two ways Müntzer is usually understood: if we take the two dimensions of his thought and work as religion and politics, then one becomes central and the other marginal. Either Müntzer was a religious thinker (and a formidable one at that) who unfortunately became mired in politics, or he was a political operator who just happened to speak in religious language. If we follow the first option, then his disagreements with Luther are theological and not political: contrary to Luther, Müntzer wanted to abolish infant baptism, he argued that the elements – bread and wine – of the Eucharist were merely emblems of Christ's sacrifice, and he espoused what he called the 'living word of God'. Unlike Luther, for whom revelation was contained in the Bible which we then need to interpret for ourselves, Müntzer believed in a continued and present revelation and prophecy. God still spoke directly with human beings, especially through visions and dreams. His favourite texts were those like Jacob's dream of the stairway to heaven (Genesis 28); Joseph's dreams, such as the one where all the ears of corn bow down to his own ear of corn, and where the stars and sun and moon bow down to worship him (Genesis 37:5–11); Solomon's dream in which he asks for wisdom from God and is granted riches and long life as well (1 Kings 3:3–15); and Peter's dream of the sheet full of all the clean and unclean animals that God commands him to eat (Acts 10:9–16). And of course dream interpreters, like Joseph or Daniel, were his favourite figures. He felt the spirit of God coursing through him, as Paul described it in his letters. These days we tend to diagnose people who claim God speaks with them as mentally unstable and quietly put them away in institutions, but that is merely another way of marginalizing those who challenge us and make us uncomfortable. In Müntzer's time it was much simpler: the rulers tortured and executed him. For Müntzer, the sign of the true minister or pastor was precisely that God used him as a prophetic vessel. Needless to say, the Catholic priests, Luther and the other reformers, and even biblical scholars fell a little short. For him, they were variously pleasure-loving pigs, devilish monks, treacherous parsons and a pack of devils.

The other way of interpreting Müntzer − as a political agitator who made use of religious language, who used the Bible for political ends − was first made by Friedrich Engels in *The Peasant War in Germany* (Marx and Engels 1975–2005: 397–482). Engels argued that Müntzer couldn't help speaking in religious and biblical terms, since it was the only language in which the peasants could voice their grievances, and since it was the dominant way of thinking about the world as such. (Later on, Ernst Bloch would pick up this line of thought in his reading of Müntzer.) This means, of course, that had Müntzer been able to use more secular and economic terms, he would have expressed the peasants' grievances in terms more familiar to us. The problem with this reading is not merely that it sidelines the role of religion in Müntzer, but that it also makes him a calculating politician. I suspect Müntzer might have lived a little longer if he had been one.

We can't really separate the political and religious elements all that easily, especially in Müntzer's situation. They are so closely intertwined it hardly makes sense to separate them at all. Are not his favoured biblical texts inescapably political? The apocalyptic texts of Daniel and Revelation promise the obliteration of the oppressive powers at God's hand, sweeping them off the face of the earth for good. In this light a long list of biblical rulers appear, from the Pharaoh in Egypt, through Ahab the King of Israel and Herod in the New Testament, to Luther himself. A continuous line runs down to Müntzer's own day, and so he too is a prophet denouncing oppression and seeking to overthrow the oppressors.

Müntzer would have been a spectacular preacher, and an inspiring leader, but I would not have liked to be under his military leadership, given that his tactical skills were a little lacking, nor indeed would I have liked to have been his wife, the former nun Ottilie von Gerson, whom he married a little less than two years before that fateful day on the battlefield at Frankenhausen. I suspect he was unbearable at home and would have tossed much in his sleep as God spoke to him in his dreams.

Gerrard Winstanley and the Diggers

Gerrard Winstanley, by contrast, would have made a good and interesting friend, if somewhat eccentric. A little naïve, especially in terms of politics, with a fondness for both writing manifestos and reading the Bible, Gerrard Winstanley was nothing less than one of the first Christian communists in the true sense of the term. He writes that 'In the beginning of Time, the great Creator Reason, made the Earth to be a Common Treasury … but not one word was spoken in the beginning, That one branch of mankind should rule over another' (Winstanley, Everard, Goodgroome et al. 1649). Class exploitation, indeed, lording it over one another in general, is simply not biblical, argues Winstanley.

Indeed, if we follow the Bible, then communist living is the only acceptable form; no masters or private property, holding everything in common. Key texts for Winstanley included Acts 4:32, or, as he paraphrases it: 'And when the Son of man, was gone from the Apostles, his Spirit descended upon the Apostles and Brethren, as they were waiting at *Jerusalem;* and Rich men sold their Possessions, and gave part to the Poor; and no man said, That ought that he possessed was his own, for they had all things Common, *Act.* 4.32' (Winstanley, Everard, Goodgroome et al. 1649). The reference to 'all things in common' also appears in Acts 2:44–5, and these texts remain central for Christian communism to the present day. But Winstanley knew his Bible, drawing together a number of texts to make a coherent programme for communist living. If Jesus said, 'if you have food and raiment, you should therewith be content' (Winstanley 1652), then we find the ideal communist life in the Garden of Eden, with the law of Moses, the government of David, and the rule of Esther, to name but a few. He also drew from Genesis 2–3 the argument that since all human beings are descended from Adam and Eve, no one is better than another for whatever reason. We are all equal before God, and there is no basis for any class distinction (especially the aristocracy). But this text from Genesis – the one of the Fall – also explained the origin of exploitation, hierarchy, the evil of monarchic rule and above all the origin of private property. The effects of the Fall must then be overcome, by means a restoration of communal life before the Fall, a restoration that began with the resurrection of Jesus Christ. In other words, what we find is a religious and political programme under the new covenant that came with Jesus Christ.

But who were the Diggers, or the 'True Levellers' as they were originally known? Coming out of a long tradition of English radicalism and inspired by the thoughts and writings of Winstanley, they formed rural communes. Moving onto common land, the Diggers dug up the land (hence their name), constructed a few buildings and then made the food from the land freely available to all. These short-lived communes embodied an effort to construct a new social order based on small egalitarian rural communities, where private property, wages and social status no longer operated.

The first Digger colony of 100–200 people was established on common land at St George's Hill, now part of Weybridge in Surrey, in 1649. They issued an open invitation for all to tear down the enclosures, come and join them and make the most of the free food, clothing and shelter available. Other communes followed in Little Heath in Surrey, Wellingborough in Northamptonshire, Iver in Buckinghamshire, and there may also have been communes in Hertfordshire, Middlesex, Bedfordshire and Gloucestershire. In each case they were there long enough to sow and harvest crops and construct buildings. The declaration by the Diggers of Wellingborough gives as good a sense as any of their aims and activities:

> A Declaration of the Grounds and Reasons why we the Poor Inhabitants of the Town of Wellingborrow, in the County of Northampton, have begun and give consent to dig up, manure and sow Corn upon

the Common, and waste ground, called Bareshanke belonging to the Inhabitants of Wellinborrow [sic], by those that have Subscribed and hundreds more that give Consent ...

... we have spent all we have, our trading is decayed, our wives and children cry for bread, our lives are a burden to us, divers of us having 5.6.7.8.9. in Family, and we cannot get bread for one of them by our labor, rich mens hearts are hardened, they will not give us if we beg at their doors; if we steal, the Law will end our lives, divers of the poor are starved to death already and it were better for us that are living to dye by the Sword then [sic] by Famine. And now we consider that the Earth is our Mother, and that God hath given it to the children of men, and that the common and waste Grounds belong to the poor, and that we have a right to the common ground both from the Law of the Land, Reason and Scriptures; and therefore we have begun to bestow our righteous labor upon it, and we shall trust the Spirit for a blessing upon our labor, resolving not to dig up any mans property, until they freely give us it ...   (Smith, Avery, Fardin et al. 1650)

Context, as always, is important. Their immediate context was the English Civil Wars (1642–51), of which the Diggers were the most radical group. Dismissing the Royalists, Parliamentary forces ('Round-heads') under the leadership of Oliver Cromwell, the Fifth Monarchy Men who wanted government placed in the hands of a returned Jesus Christ, and even the Levellers who wanted a 'level' parliament based on private property, the *True* Levellers or Diggers pushed for the abolition or 'levelling' of private property itself.

The second context is that of the long history of the enclosures. With the first stirrings of change that would later emerge as capitalism, the lords began enclosing their lands for the purpose of grazing cattle. Peasants were forced off the land and then rehired as labourers. The disorder and banditry that followed, the effort to assert the importance of private property by the extraordinary punishments (often death) for petty 'crimes' such as 'stealing' firewood or bread or hunting for food in the lord's domain, and the massive arrogance and corruption of the collapsing feudal system were all part of the social and historical context for the Diggers. They were part of the reaction

114

to the enclosures, and the great fear was that they would begin to pull down the enclosures in order to work the land. What they in fact did was cultivate the remaining commons, encouraging people, especially those dispossessed by the enclosures, to join them as the movement grew.

It hardly needs to be said that the Diggers have become the stuff of legend: communists before their time, the first hippies and counter-culture, the first greenies, seeking to live in harmony with nature, and so on. It also helps that the Diggers took a vow of non-violence, calling for the restoration of 'ancient peace and freedom', again referring to the Bible: 'He beats swords and spears into pruning hooks and ploughs; he makes both elder and younger brother freemen in the earth. Micah 4.3, 4, Isai. 33.1. and 65.17 to 25' (Winstanley 1652). They simply wanted to live in communal peace. Once the common people saw how easy it was to step out of social class, refuse to work for their lords or pay rent for the land they lived on, and to gather in self-sufficient communes, the ruling classes would wither away. Without produce from the fields or rent for their use, the aristocracy would have no choice but to disappear or join the communes. It is a beautiful, if somewhat idealistic, picture.

The neighbouring lords, however, were a little more suspicious and hard-nosed. At the original commune at St George's Hill in Surrey, the local lord of the manor – Francis Drake (not the Elizabethan admiral) – turned out to be a conservative thug (yes, they existed even then). He resorted to hiring other thugs to beat up the Diggers, and engaged an arsonist or two to burn down their buildings. Drake also took them to the courts, which then as now were stacked in favour of the powerful. The Diggers fared badly: forbidden to speak in defence, they were convicted of belonging to the Ranters – a radical and pantheistic sect that denied the authority of the Church and the Bible – and were told the army would drive them off their land if they did not leave. Winstanley protested to the Parliament, but it did little good and the Diggers left St George's Hill soon afterwards. A similar story, with local variations, appears in each of the communes: the lord of the manor used various means, both legal and illegal, to drive the Diggers out. In the face of such concerted efforts, the Digger communes were largely finished by 1651, only two years after they had begun.

As for Gerrard Winstanley, he never seems to have given up his ideals of Christian communism, although they moved him towards Quakerism in his later life. Unlike the fiery Müntzer, Winstanley (1609–76) lived to a reasonable age, especially for the time. But what is so fascinating about Winstanley are his writings, both the individual works and those he penned on behalf of the Diggers.

The man certainly loved writing, and I can envisage animated discussions lasting long into the night should I have had the chance to meet him. From *The Mysterie of God concerning the whole Creation, Mankind* in 1648 to *The Law Of Freedom in a Platform* in 1652, he wrote 23 longer and shorter pieces that have survived, from declarations and manifestos to whole books.[1] My favourites would have to be *Truth Lifting up its Head above Scandals* (1649), *An Humble Request, to the Ministers of both Universities, and to all Lawyers in every Inns-a-court* (1650) and *The True Levellers Standard ADVANCED: or, The State of Community opened, and Presented to the Sons of Men* (1649). It all makes for fascinating reading, but let me cut to the chase and identify the major themes. To begin with, like Müntzer, Winstanley's radical communist politics emerges from his reading of the Bible. It is neither a language he prefers to use, nor is the biblical material a mere add-on to the politics. For Winstanley, the Bible and radical politics are woven from one cloth. Further, Winstanley was a highly creative nonconformist who saw himself, to some extent, as part of the heritage of the Reformation. But he was very suspicious of the clergy and especially the university teachers of theology and biblical studies (with good reason, it seems). If anything, he is closer to William Blake, who had extensive contact with radical Christian groups.

Biblical texts and allusions saturate his books, the manifestos and declarations on behalf of the Diggers and the various other writings. Yet he does have his favourite texts. The story of the Fall is one, although it is a distinctly collective Fall: despite God's creation in which all are equal and have equal access to Earth's bounty, the Fall shows itself in the fact that some lord it over others; that money has come to determine human relations, creating wealth and poverty; that private property, especially in land, has arisen so as to oppress the poor; and that human relations are characterized by murder and theft. The restoration of God's will on earth, which is one with Christ's resurrection, means a restoration of the human condition before the Fall, and thus the abolition of domination, money, private property, murder and theft. As it was in the beginning, so also in England where once all shared in the 'Common Treasury', but now, especially after the Norman Conquest, oppression and land ownership prevail. This new age would be ushered in by the second Adam, who is full of love, patience, humility and righteousness, and the first, with his greed, pride, envy, power and vanity would be firmly shown out the door. Winstanley finds many texts that express such a wish, but his favoured ones are those of the prophets and the words of Jesus in the New Testament. Here he is on Christ:

> Does not Christ tell you, that if you have food and raiment, you should therewith be content? And in this common freedom, here will be food and raiment, ease and pleasure plentiful, both for you and your brethren; so that none shall beg or starve, or live in the straits of poverty – and this fulfils that righteous law of Christ, Do as you would be done by: for that law of Christ can never be performed till you establish commonwealth's freedom.   (Winstanley 1652)

In case we should miss the perpetual biblical allusions, or rather the way biblical phrases saturate his text, he is a little more explicit in the following:

> It is shewed us, That all the Prophecies, Visions, and Revelations of Scriptures, of Prophets, and Apostles, concerning the calling of the Jews, the Restauration of Israel; and making of that People, the Inheritors of the whole Earth; doth all seat themselves in this Work of making the Earth a Common Treasury; as you may read, *Ezek.* 24.26, 27, &c. *Jer.* 33.7 to 12. *Esay.* 49.17, 18, &c. *Zach.* 8. from 4, to 12, *Dan.* 2.44, 45, *Dan.* 7.27. *Hos.* 14.5, 6,7. *Joel* 2.26, 27. *Amos* 9. from 8 to the end,

Obad. 17.18.21. *Mic.* 5. from 7 to the end, *Hab.* 2.6, 7, 8, 13, 14. *Gen.* 18.18. *Rom.* 11.15. *Zeph.* 3. &c. *Zech.* 14.9.   (Winstanley 1652)

One other feature of his thought taps into a long tradition of radical biblical interpretation. It is the theory of the three ages of the world; a biblical schema of history, if you will. The first ran from Adam until Moses and was a time of murderous oppression; the second covers the period from Moses until Christ, and here we begin to see the first glimmers of a better world, such as the law of Moses and the criticisms of oppression in the prophets; the third begins with Christ and is the time of the gradual strengthening of the Spirit until all oppressive rulers can be overthrown (see especially Winstanley, Everard, Goodgroome et al. 1649).

If nothing else, this theory evokes that of Joachim of Fiore (c. 1135–1202), who divided history into the three ages of the Trinity. While the Old Testament is the 'Age of the Father' and was marked by obedience to God's law, and while the New Testament, or 'Age of the Son', is the period between Christ and the speculative year 1260 (based on Revelation 11:3 and 12:6), the 'Age of the Holy Spirit' was the end of history. This age, which was still to come, would be an age of universal love and freedom, when human beings would have direct contact with God and would finally understand the truth of Scripture. Not only would the Gospel of Christ be transcended, but so also would the Church, which would be ruled by the 'Order of the Just'.

Back to Winstanley: for all his claims to read the 'plain Text of Scripture, without exposition upon them' (Winstanley, Coulton, Palmer et al. 1649), he made extensive allegorical use of the Bible. Thus, one after another, characters and events from the Bible provide allegorical reference points for the history of England and its major historical figures. We find Adam (or A-dam), Cain and Abel, Jacob and Esau, Jonah, and so on, all lined up on the side of either the propertied and moneyed oppressors, or on the side of the poor and oppressed. Indeed, this is a refrain throughout the various texts: that he speaks on behalf of and as one of the poor oppressed people of England. What is so charming about Winstanley's writings is that these great themes from the Bible give the Diggers and common people of England the unhindered right to till, manure, sow and reap in the soil of the commons and waste lands, and like biblical people, to enjoy their bread in the sweat of their brow.

Camilo Torres and Liberation Theology

Thomas Müntzer and the Peasants' Revolt are not an isolated occurrence of radical political inspiration from the Bible. Nor are the Diggers and Gerrard Winstanley's biblical communism an aberration. A red thread runs from these radical readings to what is the greatest contemporary movement – liberation theology from the 1960s and 1970s.

Liberation theology is commonly associated with Latin America, since for particular political and economic reasons it was part of a groundswell of opposition to oppression, both local and foreign. And with the shift to the left in Latin America after the failed programmes of neo-liberal economics in the last decade or two, liberation theology is on the upsurge once again. However, let us go back to the 1960s, for out of that turbulent decade we also find liberation and political theologies springing forth in urban, Western centres of poverty and exclusion. Thus James Cone's *A Black Theology of Liberation* (1970) appeared in North America, entirely independent from the movements in Latin America. Among the Catholic Left in 1960s England – again, largely unaware of the Black and Latin American Liberation theologians – we find the circle around the journal *Slant*, which included Adrian Cunningham, Terry Eagleton, Brian Wicker, Martin Redfern and Lawrence Bright (see Cunningham et al. 1966) and the early texts of a very theological Terry Eagleton (Eagleton 1966, 1970). And in the marginal European zone of Portugal, Fernando Belo's *A Materialist Reading of the Gospel of Mark* (1981) burst on the scene. An atheist and Marxist, the self-taught Belo argues in great detail that Mark's Gospel presents Jesus as a political operator who challenges not so much the religious leaders of his time, but the Roman Imperial order

119

on behalf of the powerless. Indeed, the story of his resurrection asserts that this was one realm the Romans did not control, a mark of insurrection and source of hope for current politics. Emerging from the impetus of the resurrection, the Church (*ekklesia*) is nothing other than a revolutionary group. For Belo, 'The resurrection can only be the fruit of insurrection' (Belo 1981: 295), and he finds such a message of insurrection from the ground up in the fabric of texts such as the saying concerning the mustard seed:

> It is like a grain of mustard seed, which, when sown upon the ground, is *the smallest of all the seeds on earth*; yet when it is sown it grows up and becomes *the greatest of all shrubs, and puts forth large branches*, so that the birds of the air can make nests in its shade.   (Mark 4:31–2, emphasis added; see Belo 1981: 294)

Or the one of the growing seed:

> The kingdom is as if a man should scatter seed upon the ground, and should sleep and rise night and day, and *the seed should sprout and grow, he knows not how*. The earth produces of itself, first the blade, then the ear, then the full grain in the ear. *But when the grain is ripe* he puts in the sickle, because the harvest has come.   (Mark 4:26–9, emphasis added; see Belo 1981:294–5)

I would argue that Belo's book lies behind the subsequent reconstructions of a political Jesus that are gaining in popularity today.

However, I am most interested in the Latin American Liberation theologians. There is Gustavo Gutiérrez, who worked as a priest among the poor *barrios* of Lima, Peru, and from that experience developed the biblical notion of the 'preferential option for the poor', for which the key text is Luke 6:20, 'Blessed are you poor, for yours is the kingdom of God'. Or Jon Sobrino, writing theology from the hell of El Salvador, narrowly escaping assassination at the hands of US-backed death squads. But most fascinating, if unfortunate, is the guerrilla-priest, Camilo Torres Restrepo, who took up arms and joined the insurgent peasants in Colombia.

Torres was 37 when he was killed on 15 February 1966 by a bullet from a lone survivor of an army patrol that his guerrilla group had ambushed. It was his first engagement after joining the National Liberation Army of Colombia (*Ejército de Liberación Nacional*, or ELN). A low-ranking member of the group, he was involved in an ambush of a unit from the Colombian army with the express purpose of gaining weapons. With most of the army patrol dead, Torres broke cover and ran to grab a gun from one of the fallen soldiers. Unknown to him, a survivor of the patrol had him in his sights, and he was felled by the bullet.

Who was Camilo Torres Restrepo? He was a Roman Catholic priest, theologian and sociologist, academic, political activist and guerrilla. Indeed, he saw his move into the ELN as a natural outcome of his Christian commitment and theological study. After being ordained as priest in 1954, and having studied at the Pontifical Roman Catholic University of Leuven in Belgium, he returned to Colombia to become involved with the struggles of the oppressed poor. His stint as a university lecturer in sociology at the National University of Colombia came to an end when he finally saw that his calling as a priest was to join the rebels in 1965.

Now, usually in the various churches, the narrative of the 'call' goes something like this: God calls you to take up a form of ministry, whether that is in a parish, in a hospital or prison chaplaincy, or in some other field in which the church is involved. Or, for lay people, one may feel called to a certain profession or task, such as a missionary teacher, or nurse, and so on. Rarely does such a call include joining a guerrilla group and taking up arms. I can imagine what one's local bishop or committee for theological education might say should you front up and say just that. In other words, Camilo Torres broke ranks on the matter of the call, and his act has generated much controversy since. Should Christian clergy take up arms? Is such a call genuine? Is it is an aberration? Is it a Christian duty to overthrow the state? And so on.

The crucial point here is that Camilo Torres did not give up his religious commitment in order to join a group of Marxist-inspired guerrillas. It was not a case of either Christianity or freedom fighter: the two were for him entirely consistent, the one growing out of the other. There was certainly something in the Church's tradition and the Bible that generated such a connection for him. As a university professor, Torres was already outspoken concerning the massive divide between Colombia's rich and poor, and joining the ELN was a natural progression. Texts such as Jesus's words in Luke 12:49 and 51 were crucial: 'I came to cast fire upon the earth; and would that it were already kindled! … Do you think that I have come to give peace on earth? No, I tell you, but rather division'. Or even more strongly in Matthew:

> Do not think that I have come to bring peace on earth; I have not come to bring peace, but a sword. For I have come to set a man against his father, and a daughter against her mother, and a daughter-in-law against her mother-in-law; and a man's foes will be those of his own household. He who loves father or mother more than me is not worthy of me; and he who loves son or daughter more than me is not worthy of me; and he who does not take his cross and follow me is not worthy of me. He who finds his life will lose it, and he who loses his life for my sake will find it. (Matthew 10:34–9)

In fact, I would suggest that this may be read as a description of Torres's life, all the way from bringing a sword rather than peace, through to taking up his cross and losing his life for the sake of Christ.

The question remains, however, why he saw this option as the only one available to him at that particular moment in the 1960s. The social and economic history of Latin America was a key factor. In the wake of the populist movements in the 1950s and 1960s, such as those of Péron in Argentina and Vargas in Brazil there was a rapid modernization that took the forms of industrialization and the spread of agribusiness – multinational agricultural businesses buying land and using it for monocrops, such as coffee. That delicious smell of Brazilian or Colombian coffee in the morning is tainted with the brutal acts of the multinational companies in these years. Some benefited, especially the middle classes and urban workers, but the peasants suffered badly, either losing their land and moving to marginal lands or moving into vast shanty towns in search of work in the new industries. In response, a mass of popular movements arose, all of them with the agendas of improving the lot of the peasants. It is not for nothing that one of their platforms was land reform. In turn, the various states became military dictatorships, usually with US support, in order to protect foreign investments and the classes who benefited. In this context, the effect of the successful Cuban revolution in 1956 cannot be over-estimated: it provided a model for other liberation groups, a way of breaking from a global economic system that kept Latin American countries poor. Only now, with peak oil looming – the moment when demand exceeds supply – and oil prices skyrocketing, are the oil-rich Latin American countries gaining a stranglehold on an energy-hungry north. As they do so, the distinct history of Latin American revolutionaries has gained a new life. Chávez in Venezuela is only the best known example.

Back in 1960s Colombia, Camilo Torres experienced first-hand the desperation of the poor and dispossessed peasants and shanty town dwellers. And the National Liberation Army of Colombia offered a practical way of dealing with the massive economic dispossession of the poor. These days he would of course be dubbed a 'terrorist', the convenient catch-all for any oppositional movement. But then so would Jesus, if statements such as 'I came to cast fire upon the earth' (Luke 12:49) or 'I have not come to bring peace, but a sword' (Matthew 10:34) are anything to go by. Indeed, the ELN has been listed in the last few years as a terrorist organization by the US State Department and the European Union. However, the ELN has been operating for over 40 years, having been founded in 1964, although it is not the largest guerrilla group in Colombia (that position is held by *Fuerzas Armadas Revolucionarias de Colombia–Ejército del Pueblo* or FARC–EP with 15,000–18,000 members). In its early days, and not least because of Camilo Torres's involvement, ELN was inspired as much by liberation theology as by Marxism. The group has made Torres into an official martyr, and his example has prompted other priests to join the organization, including ELN's leader in the

1970s and 1980s, Father Manuel Pérez, or '*El Cura Pérez*'. Indeed, it was Pérez who gave shape to the group's central ideology which combined Catholic social thought, liberation theology and Marxism as part of a consistent programme to overcome systemic corruption and poverty. As I write, however, the ELN (which has its own website – www.eln-voces.com) is engaged in ongoing talks with the Colombian government aimed at dealing with ELN's concerns and moving towards reconciliation.

I wish to ask one final question: what is it about liberation theology that can lead to such guerrilla involvement? For some, Torres is an aberration, an example of the adage in Jesus's mouth, 'all who take the sword will perish by the sword' (Matthew 26:52). They seek to show that liberation theology in general is consistent with traditional Catholic teaching on social issues and point to the positive comments from the Vatican. One finds such apologies mostly from those who wish to keep a watered-down liberation theology within the confines of the church. For others, liberation theology as a whole is an aberration, an abuse of theology and a misreading of the Bible that makes it easy to dismiss. Indeed, liberation theology and its biblical interpretation generated outrage from conservative forces including the Reagan administration and the International Monetary Fund, as well as the late Pope John Paul II. During the 1980s, while John Paul II sought to drag the Roman Catholic Church into its current reactionary position, his right-hand man, Cardinal Ratzinger, berated one liberation theologian after another (before he became the next pope, Ratzinger was head of the Congregation for the Doctrine of the Faith, the successor to the Inquisition). Meanwhile, both turned a blind eye as US-backed forces systematically exterminated the leaders and members of churches that espoused liberation theology.

The scandal of the liberation theologians is to join biblical and theological reflection with Marxist social and economic analysis. And the result is an emphasis on God's preferential option for the poor, read in texts of both the Hebrew Bible and New Testament, the distinctly political elements of the Kingdom or Rule of God, the political and revolutionary dimensions of the Jesus movement, and a revolutionary ethics that challenges imperial activities. Although there is a good deal of systematic theology, especially in the work of Gustavo Gutiérrez, Juan Luis Segundo and James Cone, liberation theologians rely heavily on the Bible. The two biblical foci of liberation theology have been and remain the narrative of the Exodus in the Hebrew Bible as a continuing paradigm for political work today, as well as the figure of Jesus Christ in the New Testament, especially the close connection between salvation and liberation. If the myth of Exodus is one of release from slavery through collective and divine action, then Jesus's message was delivered to the poor, hungry, marginalized and outcast. Indeed, many liberation theologians argue for a revolutionary core to the Bible with its systematic criticism of poverty and oppression.

Yet liberation theologians have always held Marxism at a distance, limiting its use to analysing capitalism, especially the social, political and economic dimensions of oppression and exploitation. I, for one, would prefer a much greater engagement with Marx, but the main reason that the liberation theologians do not do so is to avoid idolatry by means of an ontological reserve. They argue that without some form of divine transcendence, one cannot avoid idolizing what is human. The polemic of Isaiah against idols still has bite: 'All who make idols are nothing, and the things they delight in do not profit … Who fashions a god or casts an image, that is profitable for nothing?' (Isaiah 44:9–10). So the only perspective that avoids idolatry, the raising of human beings or the products of human hands into the status of gods, is the figure of God (ontological transcendence). And this includes Marxism, the proletariat, or indeed the leader of the movement. The problem with such an argument is that 'God' does not quite sidestep the same trap of idolatry, unless one brings in a true–false dichotomy: 'God' is true, but other gods are false. Be that as it may, some proponents of liberation theology, such as Jon Sobrino and José Miranda, argue that one can arrive at the insights of liberation theology out of the Christian tradition and the Bible, without necessary recourse to Marxism. With or without Marxism, what the liberation theologians do manage to show in their work is the inescapably *political* nature of the Bible.

125

Liberation theology became a default position for many on the Christian left, and people began applying its insights to feminism, indigenous readings of the Bible, ecological readings, queer interpretation and so on. But as my third example of the way the Bible gives rise to radical political readings and actions, liberation theology for all its shortcomings constitutes the most influential contemporary movement of the religious left.

Conclusion

The examples I have chosen – Thomas Müntzer and the Peasants' Revolt, Gerrard Winstanley and the Diggers, and Camilo Torres and liberation theology – are but three moments in the history of revolutionary readings of the Bible. There are many more examples I might have given, such as the International League of Religious Socialists, which has over 200,000 members and represents religious socialist movements in 21 countries and across a number of religions (www.ilrs.org); or Étienne Cabet (1788–1856), who, arguing that communism is in fact pure Christianity, left France to establish socialist or 'Icarian' communities in the United States; or Father Thomas J. Haggerty, a Marxist Roman Catholic priest and founder of the Industrial Workers of the World (the 'Wobblies'); or the noted New Testament scholar, Richard Horsley, who is developing a comprehensive picture of the economic and political climate in which the revolutionary Jesus movement took shape; or Martin Buber, who espoused an influential form of Jewish spirituality and philosophy while at the same time holding to a socialist political agenda; or Hugo Chávez, the president of Venezuela and scourge of the United States, who pointed out recently: 'Capitalism is the way of the devil and exploitation. If you really want to look at things through the eyes of Jesus Christ – who I think was the first socialist – only socialism can really create a genuine society' (Padget 2006).

I leave it to readers to remember and explore other examples. But the whole point of my exploration of Müntzer, Winstanley and Torres has been to bring to the fore this tradition in which the Bible has provided the content, substance and motivation for left revolutions. In the end, it matters little whether one thinks that the Bible provided and provides a distinct language in which to express political and economic concerns, or whether its status as a sacred text (for some) provides an extra impetus. What does matter is that this collection of texts, for all its faults and shortcomings, continues to be part of the construction of a revolutionary worldview.

6

Rescuing the Bible

Thesis Six: The Bible is one source for a political myth for the worldly left, a political myth that, while keeping in mind the perpetual need for theological suspicion, condemns oppression, imagines a better society and draws deeply on the mythic images of rebellious chaos.

Introduction: Constructing a Political Myth

One question remains: what can a worldly left retrieve from the Bible? It seems to me that crucial elements from the Bible may contribute to what I call a 'political myth' for the left – elements such as the condemnation of oppression, imagining a communist society and a recovery of the theme of mythic chaos. By 'myth' I mean an alternative language, one that is saturated with images and metaphors, one that we use to speak about what cannot be spoken of in everyday terms. By 'political myth' I mean a political vision or an image of the future that uses the imagery and language of myth. The Bible is, it seems to me, one resource for such visions and images, since it is, after all, a vast storehouse of utopian themes, with religious, social and political ideas running across and through one another. However, any use of the Bible in this way needs a good dose of theological suspicion, especially since theological suspicion cuts down any tendency to reifying and idolizing saviour figures, leaders and movements. In what follows, then, I return to the question of theological suspicion

128

before providing some of the building blocks that may be drawn from the Bible for a political myth for the worldly left.

In the politics of alliance that I have named the worldly left, the old suspicion of myth that is still widespread among the old secular left needs to be jettisoned, not least because the left has in the past been rather busy constructing its own political myths. The new Soviet man and woman is one: young, strong and industrious, they were also chaste and virtuous. Plastered over walls in giant posters, or idealized in Soviet Realist novels, the new man and woman embodied the vigour and freshness of the new Russia after the Revolution. Another political myth is Georges Sorel's general strike, which he pushed as a motivational device at the turn of the nineteenth and twentieth centuries. If the efforts to outlaw the general strike and wind down or limit strike action as such are anything to go by, the general strike can still strike fear into employers and governments, and even the population at large, who panic and stock up on flour, milk and sugar. I would also suggest that the idea of the Revolution has a deep mythic structure. The French, Russian and Chinese Revolutions have become the stuff of myth, as have, to a lesser extent, the English (i.e. the Civil War) and American Revolutions. This is not to say that such myths have become purely positive, since their legacy remains ambivalent – at least, depending upon whom you speak to. But the call for revolution is still a strong political myth, especially among broad swathes of the left.

I can push this even further. It is an old point, but one worth repeating: there is a deeply biblical current running in Marxist critiques of oppression and calls for a revolution to a new economic order. One may easily make the same point concerning anarchist political myths, especially the deep suspicion of and desire to be rid of the state and its various oppressive appurtenances. In many circumstances, this observation counts as a dismissal – the left is merely offering another religion in place of the ones it rejects. On the contrary, for it seems to me one of the great appeals of the left is its ability to generate powerful and persuasive myths, an ability that it shares with religion, and particularly the Bible. It also means that my task of suggesting some contributions from the Bible is somewhat easier.

I will turn to that task in a moment, but the affinity between the left and the Bible is perhaps best captured by two anecdotes, one apocryphal and the other less so. It is not so well known that when Marx and Engels wrote the *Communist Manifesto* they did so at the request of a group that had not long beforehand been known as the League of the Just. The curious thing about the League of the Just, which had been formed in 1836, was that it was an organization with a substantial religious flavour. Not only did it propagate utopian socialist and communist ideas and practices on the basis of the Bible, but it was also soon to become the first international communist organization. Marx and Engels joined it in 1847 and were influential in changing its name to the Communist League. The old slogan of the League of the Just was distinctly biblical: it was to be 'based on the ideals of love of one's neighbour, equality and justice'.

Now for the more apocryphal story (one that I have used before), which was told to me by an old professor of theology who had an uncanny resemblance to Karl Marx. One Sunday morning, Jenny was setting off for church with the children from their tiny London flat (in Soho). Marx of course was not going, although perhaps he should have been, working away on one or other of his great books. But as they walked out of the front door, he growled, 'You'd be better off reading the Hebrew prophets!'

A Note on Theological Suspicion

In the first chapter I mentioned briefly the importance of theological suspicion in the programme of a new secularism for biblical studies. The main purpose of theological suspicion, which I have discussed in detail elsewhere (Boer 2007a), is to defuse the tendency to giving an object, idea or person a role in salvation, or turning them into quasi-divinities. This process happens all too often in political movements. It appears when an individual becomes a great leader who will save us, often achieving semi-divine or divine status, with the usual adoration and worship upon death or even beforehand. It may also be a group that bears this saving role, whether that is the revolutionary cadre, or the chosen people, or the Church, or the state. Another name for such a process is the messiah complex or the search for a redeemer figure. It may be a particular programme, and we have plenty of these from which to choose – a religious sect that claims to hold the truth, or a small political group that is the bearer of the revolutionary seed, or the state with all of its patriotism and nationalism, or indeed an economic programme that believes blindly that the market will save us if only we stop hindering it and give it free reign.

The Bible is full of such tendencies, with its ideal figures such as Abraham, Moses, Jesus, Paul, or indeed 'God', whose reputed words are pored over and mined for their meaning. Political movements too, in the continuum of the left and right, have such a tendency – I need only mention the reverence for Marx and his written word, or Adam Smith and his *The Wealth of Nations*, or Hitler and *Mein Kampf*, or Mao Zedung and his *Little Red Book*, or the Bible itself, whose words one must revere and about which one must not make jokes. Indeed, it was not so long ago that blasphemy was a criminal offence for which one might be rewarded with a short, sharp spell in prison.[1] In each case a crucial signal of such idolatry is that the person and text has been revered and reviled, worshipped and condemned. Indeed, in a more biblical sense, theological suspicion is also the critique of idolatry, blocking the overwhelming drive to make an object of worship out of material things and human figures.

Finally, theological suspicion is another form of the Marxist practice of ideological suspicion. In its old sense, ideological suspicion seeks to unmask what is in the end propaganda. Thus when one group claims that a particular act or programme is good for you, ideological suspicion seeks to show that such a claim actually justifies oppression. For example, the move to drive down wages, break the unions and improve profits for large transnationals is presented as providing the opportunity for an increase in wages and the power of individual workers to bargain for better conditions. Or the old reactionary role of the Church in urging people to put up with exploitation and not protest and revolt since they will be rewarded in heaven for their faithfulness is actually a means of ensuring that the powers that be remain untroubled. Or the claim by the Church that we must accept each other in love, because God is love, may in fact be a way of ensuring that nothing changes. We accept you as you are, it goes, but that means we don't have to do anything about the system that makes you poor or rich, sick or healthy, exploiter or exploited. Or the claim to be a victim of past oppression may be used to justify the oppression of others in the name of survival, as we see on both sides of the conflict in the Middle East between Israelis and Palestinians. It seems to me that there is still a distinct role for such ideological suspicion, or demystification as it is sometimes called, especially in any political myth. I would hope that the elements of a political myth that I am about to outline avoids being a justification for yet some other form of oppression, as well as avoiding the drive to reify and idolize a figure or movement. In short, any political myth worth its name should be subject to both theological suspicion and ideological suspicion.

A Political Myth

However, what texts are worth using for such a myth? What texts, in other words, are worth rescuing from the right? We might group them roughly into condemnations of economic exploitation, images of collective or communist living, and those powerful mythical themes of chaos. The first two are not particularly new, being the stuff of the movements I discussed in the preceding chapter – the Peasants' Revolt and Müntzer, the Diggers and Winstanley, and liberation theology and Torres. Indeed, we would be hard put to find a revolutionary movement inspired by the Bible that has not made use of these first two themes. All the same, I think they are worth retrieving. However, I must admit to a liking for the last theme – the texts of chaos – since they have been used far less often. I like these biblical texts of chaos because they focus on disruption and its threat, on the process of breakdown and change, rather than on any result. I also like them, since chaos is almost always cast in the Bible as a negative feature, something to be overcome through order and control. In this respect the biblical opposition is like that old spoof of the Cold War called *Get Smart*. In that television series, the two opposing forces of Good and Evil, of Communism and Capitalism were stripped down to the conflict between 'Control' and 'Kaos'. Not only did I always sympathize with the side of Kaos, but Control, with its frustrated Chief and dim-witted agent Maxwell Smart, always seemed to be in more chaos than Kaos itself.

Let me repeat a point I made earlier: the texts that follow deal in images and metaphors, rather than any concrete descriptions or blueprints. Not only is this also what appeals to me about them, but it is the stuff of myth itself.

Critiquing oppression

The condemnations of injustice and oppression have been and remain the staple of the religious left. They are found in diverse places throughout the Bible, in the mouths of Moses, the prophets and Jesus, turning up in surprising corners of the law and other places. These texts still ring out for those who seek motivation for condemning the differentiation and injustices of wealth, power and privilege. However, in calling upon these texts, we need to exercise some theological suspicion, especially when the story of one's own oppression becomes the justification for oppressing others. I will have more to say on this point as I move along, but it is important to build theological suspicion into the myths themselves.

The most sustained critiques are placed by the unknown authors of the Bible in the mouths of prophets. I give an example or two before discussing them more fully.

> Woe to those who decree iniquitous decrees,
>   and the writers who keep writing oppression,
> to turn aside the needy from justice
>   and to rob the poor of my people of their right,
> that widows may be their spoil,

133

> and that they may make the fatherless their prey!
> What will you do on the day of punishment,
>   in the storm which will come from afar?
> To whom will you flee for help,
>   and where will you leave your wealth?
>   (Isaiah 10:1–3)

This passage – and there are many others like it – come from the collection of sayings known as the book of Isaiah. In this passage the law-givers and writers (of the law) come in for a beating for encoding injustice into the laws. We really do not have to look to our own time to realize that the law, no matter how much it is supposed to be impartial and above economics or politics, usually ends up serving someone's interests. The law is anything but disinterested. Here the laws in question go against the needy, the poor, widows and orphans (the fatherless) – a rather traditional gathering of vulnerable groups in these texts. Hardly any surprise here; nor should it be any surprise that the laws favour the wealthy and powerful. As far as the text is concerned, it is precisely these people who will pay for their corruption. Just when they thought they had it their way, when they had managed to craft the laws in their favour, Yahweh comes in to offer his judgement and punishment. Then there will be no patron on whom to rely, and their wealth will not help them in the least.

The book of Isaiah has had all manner of theories thrown at it. One of course is that there actually was a prophet called Isaiah who lived in the eighth century BCE who predicted events well in the future, including the Babylonian exile and return from it in the sixth century BCE. Another theory is that what we have are sayings from at least three different figures at different times, one in the eighth, another in the sixth and then another even later. The reason for gathering the various pieces – usually broken up into chapters 1–39, 40–55 and 56–66 – is that they came from an 'Isaianic school' that carried on in the spirit of its founder. Others have challenged the possibility that anyone known as Isaiah actually lived, since all we know about him comes from this collection. Thus the figure of Isaiah is a product of the texts that happen to bear his name. According to this approach, the collection of sayings attributed to Isaiah is really a much later text and the largely fictional and legendary character 'Isaiah' happened to be a convenient and authoritative peg on which to hang these sayings. Finally, some have questioned whether these prophetic texts really are so much on the side of the poor and oppressed. Might it not be that taking up the cause of the poor is one strategy for an alternative political programme, in much the same way that politicians will appeal to the ordinary, everyday voter – the average Joe?

For some strange reason, the effect of the words has not been diminished by any of these theories. It seems to matter little whether there was a prophet called Isaiah, or whether he is a purely fictional creation of later scribes, or whether the texts mask another intention that is not so radical after all: what actually counts are the words themselves. And they have been used time and again to condemn anyone who grinds the poor and needy into the ground.

Here is another text from Isaiah that works on the same theme:

> The Lord enters into judgement
>   with the elders and princes of his people:
> 'It is you who have devoured the vineyard,
>   and the spoil of the poor is in your houses.
> 'What do you mean by crushing my people,
>   by grinding the face of the poor?'
>   says the Lord God of hosts.
>
> (Isaiah 3:14–15)

Here it is the elders and princes, or perhaps more accurately elders and chieftains, who are the guilty ones. It is precisely those who command and demand honour – whether through age or power – who are at fault. Notice here that 'the people' and 'the poor' merge with one another: 'What do you mean by crushing my people / by grinding the face of the poor?' That long recognized pattern of parallelism – in which two lines say the same things in different ways – ensures such a link. We can go two ways in interpreting these two lines. Firstly, the 'poor' are actually the whole 'people': all of them, not merely a section or part, have suffered at the hands of the elders and chieftains. Secondly, we may go the other way, and suggest that the 'poor' are really God's people, 'my people'. Either way, as far as the text is concerned, the effect is to condemn those with the reigns of power and honour.

Texts such as Isaiah 3:14–15 are central to liberation theology's tenet of the 'preferential option for the poor'. More explicitly, liberation theologians argue that God is a God of the poor. However, this is where things become tricky, since it borders on the idea of a 'chosen people', and we need to exercise some theological suspicion. Before we know it, we have the beginnings of the identification of a certain group that becomes the key to salvation. In other words, it becomes an idol to be revered, and it doesn't help matters that God is connected directly with that chosen people, the poor. In order to avoid such a move, I suggest that the exposing and condemning of oppression is crucial to any political myth, but that any move to identify a chosen group plays dangerously with a tendency to idolatry and therefore needs to be recognized and blocked.

Another prophetic figure (who, like Isaiah, may have existed or may be a product of a scribe's literary imagination) who fires off some forceful condemnations is Amos. For example:

Thus says the Lord:
'For three transgressions of Israel,
and for four, I will not revoke the punishment;
because they sell the righteous for silver,
    and the needy for a pair of shoes –
they that trample the head of the poor into the dust of the earth …'.
(Amos 2:6–7)

Another version of the image we encountered earlier with Isaiah also turns up here: crushing and grinding the face of the poor in Isaiah here become the trampling of the poor into the dust. Here the condemnation concerns the selling of the righteous and the needy. Is the reference to slavery, especially debt slavery? Possibly, but notice again how the 'righteous' and the 'needy' merge into one another: 'they sell the righteous for silver / and the needy for a pair of shoes'. 'Righteous' is an unfortunate translation, since it has taken on the sense of someone who is overly pious or self-righteous. So perhaps the 'just' would be better, or (my own preference) the 'uncorrupted', those who do not engage in corrupt and deceitful practices. Indeed, another text from Amos spells out such corruption and deceit in some detail:

> Hear this, you who trample upon the needy,
>   and bring the poor of the land to an end,
> saying 'When will the new moon be over,
>   that we may sell grain?
> And the Sabbath,
>   that we may offer wheat for sale,
> that we may make the ephah small and the shekel great,
>   and deal deceitfully with false balances,
> that we may buy the poor for silver
>   and the needy for a pair of sandals,
>   and sell the refuse of the wheat.
>
> (Amos 8:4–6)

Keen to get past the waste of time that is a religious festival, the corrupt deal in false weights (reducing the ephah) by means of false balances, sell waste products as though they were the real thing (the refuse of the wheat), so that they can take even more from the poor and needy. The desired outcome is the same – being able to bring the poor and needy into debt slavery.

There is much more in this vein throughout the prophetic material: denunciation of oppression, condemnation of economic exploitation and so on. These texts and others were the ones that fired up Thomas Müntzer, Gerrard Winstanley and the liberation theologians, to mention but a few. It is important to keep the economic and social focus of these texts: they expose and decry economic and social exploitation. I write this, since every now and then they are read in spiritual or ecclesiastical senses. In this light, the poor and needy become the faithful who suffer at the hands of the unbelieving world. All the faithful need do is hold fast, for God is on their side. Or, on a more ecclesiastical note, the oppressors are part of an obscenely wealthy Church that exploits ignorant common people. This was a position the Reformers took, casting themselves in the role of prophets with God on their side against a corrupt Church. The trap with such approaches to these texts is one I have already flagged: the connection with God all too easily removes these condemnations from their economic and social location. It is, in other words, another moment for theological suspicion to do its work. Since God is the locus of justice in these texts, it is all too easy to use that connection with God to remove the economic and social matrix of these condemnations and move them into spiritual and ecclesiastical spheres.

Apart from the prophetic materials, there are other places in the Bible where economic and social oppression are also condemned. These too cannot be ignored in any sustainable political myth for a worldly left. No matter how much Moses turns out to be the autocrat who relies on his divine right, the figure who stands and calls on Pharaoh to 'let my people go' (Exodus 5:1) remains a crucial feature of a political myth. The ambivalence concerning Moses – is he a liberator or an autocrat – is more important than we might think, since he brings home the need to build theological suspicion into any political myth. The ambivalence over Moses is ambivalence over freedom: too often freedom means not merely freedom *from* oppression, but also freedom *for* oppression.[2] Too often those who were the victims of oppression use that story to justify oppressing others. Here lies the importance of Moses: apart from treating him as a saviour figure, the narrative of the Exodus that moves from Egypt to the conquest of the Promised Land is a paradigmatic text for the way freedom may be abused and distorted. In other words, any call for freedom, any call to 'let my people go' must guard against using such a call as the basis for oppressing others.

Then there are the New Testament texts, especially the reputed words of Jesus in which he condemns the rich and powerful, is anti-establishment and anti-clerical, identifies with the poor and oppressed, lives a communal life with the disciples who gave up all to join the group. Well-known sayings still have bite, such as, 'It is easier for a camel to go through the eye of a needle than for a rich man to enter the kingdom of God' (Mark 10:25). Or the words of the Son of Man,

138

when he identifies with the poor and hungry in the parable of the sheep and the goats: 'I was hungry and you gave me food, I was thirsty and you gave me drink, I was a stranger and you welcomed me, I was naked and you clothed me, I was sick and you visited me, I was in prison and you came to me' (Matthew 25:35–6).

I could add even more examples, such as the law texts that ensure the foreigner is welcomed and treated well. The call to 'love the foreigner', rather than give a racist or xenophobic response, remains a challenge (Deuteronomy 10:18–19). But I have provided enough here to show that the uncovering and condemnation of oppression runs deep in the Bible. Such condemnation is what the old secular left and the religious left share at a deep level, so it should come as no surprise that I suggest it should also be a part of any myth for the worldly left.

However, the consequences of such condemnations can be ambivalent, as the stories that cluster around Moses show only too well. The victim can all too easily become the oppressor; the story of suffering oppression can become the story that justifies oppressing others. The way to block such a process is to include these stories too within any political myth, even if it is only as negative examples of what to avoid. Further, it is all too easy for texts such as the Bible to lift off from the social and economic base of oppression and turn it into some spiritual or religious affair. Any such spiritualizing will have to face up to theological suspicion, for it seems to me that theological suspicion should be built into any political myth where exploitation and oppression are the focus. It is all very well to denounce and condemn systematic oppression, marching on the streets, waving flags, shouting slogans, blockading the police, and tearing down fences and governments – activities that have become synonymous with the left – but without blocking the way those condemnations turn into oppression themselves, we are back where we started.

Images of collective living

The second great theme that emerges from the Bible is that of communal or communist living – understood in the original sense of the term. Now we are right in the midst of image and metaphor, in the midst of myth itself, since it is impossible to speak about these matters in everyday terms, or in the precise language of science, or in any matter-of-fact terms. The reason I make this point is that we are dealing with a better society and a better life, what I would want to call in the best sense of the term, utopian. Since, by definition, those societies are qualitatively different from our own, it becomes impossible to use the language of what we know to speak about what we can only dimly perceive. Thus the language of myth is far more appropriate, and the Bible has a vast reservoir of such language.

At this point the cynic in me mutters about pies in the sky, about futile and often brutal schemes for the improvement of the human lot, whether those are of Hitler or Mussolini, or Stalin or Pol Pot, or Milton Friedman (2002) and Friedrich von Hayek (1960) and the dreams of a capitalist utopia whose ruins we see everywhere around us. Do they too not have their myths which they believed would achieve the ideal community? Once again, this is where any worthwhile political myth risks collapsing if it does not include such negative moments in its reckoning, for utopia can all too quickly turn into dystopia.

With that in mind, I am interested in the enduring power of the image of communal living that appears in the Acts of the Apostles. This has been a founding and enabling myth for Christian communism. It comes from Acts 2:44–5: 'And all who believed were together and had all things in common; and they sold their possessions and goods and distributed them to all, as any had need.' As we saw earlier, this was a crucial text for the Diggers and Gerrard Winstanley, as was Acts 4:32–5 with its talk of having everything in common and the distribution to any who had need:

> Now the company of all those who believed were of one heart and soul, and no one said that any of the things which he possessed was his own, but they had everything in common. And with great power the apostles gave their testimony to the resurrection of the Lord Jesus, and great grace was upon them all. There was not a needy person among them, for as many as were possessors of lands or houses sold them, and

brought the proceeds of what was sold and laid it at the apostles' feet; and distribution was made to each as any had need.

Among many others, this founding myth inspired Étienne Cabet, who argued that communism is in fact pure Christianity. Cabet (1788–1856) was a fiery character and endeared himself neither to the Roman Catholic hierarchy nor the French Government. Soon enough, the deeply Christian but anti-clerical Cabet was found guilty of treason and fled France. In his later years he attempted to establish socialist – or 'Icarian' as he called them – communities in the United States, basing them on the model of his 1840 book *Travel and Adventures of Lord William Carisdall in Icaria* (*Voyage et aventures de lord William Carisdall en Icarie*).

I wrote above 'founding myth', for although many have taken these texts as a description of the actual practice of the first Christian communities, the book of Acts is as unreliable as any biblical text for historical data. Here we face delightful contradiction: the less historically reliable such a story is, the more powerful it is as a political myth. In fact, it is important to insist that this picture of the early Christian community rests on the flimsiest of evidence – the book of Acts – since only then can we avoid the tendency of trying to restore some pristine state that has been disrupted by a 'fall'. As long as the belief holds that Acts presents what was once a real, lived experience, the more efforts to restore that ideal early Church become reactionary. For any effort at restoring what was lost, of overcoming a 'fall', is reactionary in the first degree. Such efforts have bedevilled movements within the Church over two millennia, movements that have sought in their own ways to return to that first community. I have of course been engaging in another moment of theological suspicion, for what happens in these efforts is that the mythical early Church becomes a desirable point of origin that needs to be retrieved. However, if we insist that the communal life of the early Church is myth, that it projects a wish as to what might be, that it gives us a powerful image of what may still be achieved, then we are able to overcome the reactionary desire to return to the early Church in the book of Acts. Then we are able to reclaim it as a radical rather than a reactionary agenda.

Even more, it is a rather flawed myth – all the better to my mind. Early Marxists were rather taken with this myth of the early Church, arguing that it represents a deeper current of communism within Christianity. However, the likes of Karl Kautsky (1958) and Rosa Luxemburg (1905) also pointed out that what we have in Acts is a communism of consumption rather than production. It is all very well for people to aspire – based on the stories in Acts – to share everything, to sell all they have and own it communally. But that does nothing to change the way such things are produced. What happens when the goods run out? Do people go back to their various professions in order to produce or buy more goods so that they can sell them again or share them once more? Kautsky and Luxemburg pointed out that the picture in Acts is a good first step, but that it needs much more, namely a change in the economic system to sustain any form of communal living.

A stronger mythical image of what is required for communal life comes from the Hebrew Bible:

> What does the Lord require of you
> but to do justice, and to love kindness,
>   and to walk humbly with your God?
> (Micah 6:8)

Now, while this may seem rather simple, doing justice, loving kindness and walking humbly comprise an extremely tall order for any collective, or indeed individual, life. It is not for nothing that this text has been and remains a slogan for many on the religious left. However, what these three items entail is spelled out a little more in the following:

> The Spirit of the Lord God is upon me,
>   because the Lord has anointed me
> to bring good tidings to the poor;
>   he has sent me to bind up the brokenhearted,
> to proclaim liberty to the captives,
>   and the opening of the prison to those who are bound;
> to proclaim the year of the Lord's favour,
>   and the day of vengeance of our God.
>   (Isaiah 61:1–2; RSV, translation modified)

142

This text might be read as a direct follow-on from the condemnations of oppression I discussed in the previous section. Here the captives are to be set free, the prisoners released, the poor and broken-hearted to hear good news. Not quite a detailed programme for reform, but then it is a poetic text and it would be enough to send an earthquake or two through any vested power. It does, however, hint at what is required for any viable collective living, namely the end of exploitation and oppression, and that is a substantial and revolutionary move. It is not for nothing that the Gospel of Luke places this text in the mouth of Jesus when he is in the synagogue in Nazareth (Luke 4:18–19).

Out of many other possibilities, there is a further text concerning the image of collective life that I would like to quote and explore:

> Then the eyes of the blind shall be opened,
>   and the ears of the deaf unstopped;
> then shall the lame man leap like a hart,
>   and the tongue of the dumb sing for joy.
> For waters shall break forth in the wilderness,
>   and streams in the desert;
> the burning sand shall become a pool,
>   and the thirsty ground springs of water.
>   (Isaiah 35:5–7)

I have chosen this text for two reasons. Firstly, it introduces the image of healing, and secondly, it moves out of the closed circle of human concerns. As for the first point, a text like this – in which the deaf, blind, lame and dumb will be able to hear, see, walk and talk – fires up all manner of associations. And each association seems to enhance the text's metaphors, to show how deeply this wish runs. For example, the suggestion that in this text the human body with all its ailments is really a metaphor for human society strengthens the metaphoric power of the text. Even more, one common Christian move is to appropriate this text and others like it as images of heaven, but this is merely another way to emphasize its utopian appeal. What do these metaphors suggest? Is it physical healing? But that then makes the deaf, blind, lame and dumb incomplete human beings until they are healed. Is it social or political or economic healing? Is it an existential desire? Or is it a collective wish for a community that has not yet been experienced in full?

Let me pick up the second element of the quotation from Isaiah 35:5–7, namely, its move outside strictly human concerns. Now, this is where myth really does push the boundaries of the imagination, for most images of utopian societies are overwhelmingly anthropocentric, where human beings may live in 'harmony' with nature but nothing much more. But what happens when human beings are not so central, when human beings are merely one in a number? This possibility trades in part on the imagery of the Garden of Eden, although that still has human beings at the pinnacle and centre of paradise. What if human beings are not so central after all? One or two texts hint at this possibility:

> My beloved speaks and says to me:
> 'Arise, my love, my fair one,
>   and come away;
> for lo, the winter is past,
>   the rain is over and gone.
> The flowers appear on the earth,
>   the time of singing has come,
> and the voice of the turtledove
>   is heard in our land.
> The fig tree puts forth its figs,
>   and the vines are in blossom;
>   they give forth fragrance.
> Arise, my love, my fair one, and come away.'   (Song 2:10–13)

> The wolf shall dwell with the lamb,
>   and the leopard shall lie down with the kid,
> and the calf and the lion and the fatling together,
>   and a little child shall lead them.
> The cow and the bear shall feed;
>   their young shall lie down together;
>   and the lion shall eat straw like the ox.
> The sucking child shall play over the hole of the asp,
>   and the weaned child shall put his hand on the adder's den.
>   (Isaiah 11:6–8)

144

These are nothing other than a very different communal living. Heavily metaphorical, deeply mythical, but they too should be part of a political myth for a worldly left.

Before I get carried away in some ecotopian mysticism, I would like to return to the problem with which I began this section. What about the cynic's response that all such dreams of collective life, the ideal community and paradise on earth almost always turn sour and become oppressive? The immediate answer to this question is that myths of utopia are fine when they are open and exploratory, but when you actually get to the point of creating a community, you need an authoritarian act of closure. Someone has to make that decision of closure: the boundaries must be set, the rules established, especially concerning decisions as to who may be admitted and who not. At this point, utopia becomes dystopia, and all those fears of utopian dreaming come to the fore. In this situation, the advantage of the myths of collective life that I have drawn upon is that they are open-ended. They are myths, not blueprints and plans, not objects to adore, and therefore their function is to embody dreams and hopes, act as inspiration and motivation.

At this point I want to bring in my second answer, which actually undermines the first. For I would like to go further and ask whether it is really necessary for actual collective life to bring about some sort of closure. Indeed, there have been and are many collective experiments that have worked, even for a short time. They are both relatively small-scale and local, and they are often far more complex than anything most of us have experienced. And their overwhelming experience is that they throw up all manner of new problems that need to be dealt with. But that is as it should be, it seems to me, for the need to work out those problems is part of that new experiment. In their infinite complexity, the need to deal with ongoing questions and problems, indeed to come to an end and start anew, is there not a perpetual openness? In this context, perhaps these words from Isaiah are an appropriate slogan:

> Behold, the former things have come to pass,
> and new things I now declare;

145

before they spring forth
I tell you of them.
(Isaiah 42:9)

Reclaiming chaos

The final theme that may become part of such a political myth is one of chaos. In particular, it seems to me that one of the most promising items is the connection between natural chaos and human rebellion that shows up in the biblical material with surprising frequency. This effort to recover the connection between chaos and rebellion is also rather appealing since it is an act of theological suspicion in itself. I don't need to incorporate theological suspicion into this theme, as I did with the condemnation of oppression and images of a communist society. Rather, in giving space to, indeed in recovering, the themes of chaos and rebellion, I am recovering what is almost uniformly cast in the negative, what is almost always condemned in the biblical stories themselves. It is an act of theological suspicion because I am suspicious as to why chaos is put in terms of a threat to divine and human order, and why rebellion is so often cast as rebellion against God and against rulers who claim to be appointed by God.

Here I dig into one of the most basic oppositions of mythology – that between chaos and order. However, in valorizing chaos, I also cut against the grain of the vast majority of myths and their interpretations, for a basic feature of myth is that it tells the story of the victory of order over chaos. That order takes many forms, such as the creation of the natural world with its regions and cycles, or the establishment of society with its structures, such as classes, genders, government, law, priestly ritual and so on. Often the establishment of order involves the establishment of a city with its divinely appointed king, as we find in the Babylonian creation myth *Enuma Elish*. Often it involves a primal conflict between the forces of chaos (usually watery and female) and those of order (usually male and firm and solid). Above all, chaos is a negative in these myths, and order unquestionably desirable. It seems to me that chaos is what actually needs to be retrieved from

146

the mythology of the Bible. In other words, there is much greater potential in the biblical themes of chaos, darkness and the wild realm of nature than in the old staples of order, light and civilization.

Let me give a few examples. To begin with, in the first chapter of Genesis, we find a classic cosmogonic myth in which the problem is that the earth is 'without form and void' (*tohu wavohu* in Genesis 1:2). All we have is a darkness that covers 'the deep' (*tehom*, Genesis 1:2). Everything about the story from here on concerns the effort to order and arrange this formless void of the deep. Not only does it proceed by the somewhat artificial ordering of time in terms of days of the week, but a series of divisions follows: between light and darkness as Night and Day, between the waters above and below, and between Earth and Sea. Once these divisions have been made, we can then have vegetation on the Earth, lights in the sky to order time and seasons, and living creatures in the sky, sea and on the earth. Last but not least, human beings appear, separate from the rest of the created order, but the ones who also are to have dominion over it. Apart from the need to have creation clearly demarcated, with its boundaries and accepted zones, the whole process involves an incessant naming – Day, Night, Sky, Earth, and Seas – which is yet another effort to assert order.

But what if we take sides not with the order of this myth but its chaos? What if we prefer the formless void and the darkness of the deep over against the obsessive desire for order and control?[3] The mythic possibilities of such a preference show up in another story in these early chapters of Genesis, namely that of the Flood (Genesis 6–9). Here chaos turns up with renewed vigour in the flood that engulfs the earth: 'all the fountains of the great deep burst forth, and the windows of the heavens were opened' (Gen. 7:11). Our friend, the 'deep', has returned. Indeed, the verse echoes the second day of creation, except in reverse. There, God separates the waters that were under the firmament that is called 'Sky' and those that were above it (Gen. 1:6–8). Here, in the flood, that neat separation bursts asunder and the waters rush to meet one another again, released from their confinement in joyous chaos. For the flood story, the only point of order is the boat itself, where the carefully numbered animals join with the

147

clan of Noah. By the end of the story, order will be restored and the vast chaotic flood will have ebbed.

In the meantime, however, a crucial connection has been made: human 'sin' makes an alliance with natural chaos. Recognizing such a connection entails that we do two things. Firstly, an option for chaos is an option against a God of order and control, a God of the palace guard and secret police. Secondly, in making such a move, we need to valorize the negative, or at least what is cast as negative in some of the biblical texts. Once we have done so, the natural chaos and political chaos merge and mingle with another. In fact, natural chaos is a code for human rebellion and vice versa. Notice what happens in the story: the human depravity and corruption of the first verses of chapter 6, amongst whom Noah stands out as something of a pain, become the direct cause of the natural chaos of the flood. In both cases, human rebellion and natural chaos break out of the regulation and control that God tries to exercise: while the thoughts of human hearts were 'only evil continually' (Gen. 6:5), the flood sends everything into flux at the first opportunity. Even more, it is because of human depravity that the earth itself became corrupt, and so it all had to be destroyed (Gen. 6:7, 11–12).

Once this connection has been made, my final and favourite example begins to look somewhat different – the Murmuring Stories of the Wilderness Wanderings. I have mentioned the rebellion of Korah of Numbers 16 at an earlier point, but here it is worth pointing out another feature of that story. After the rebellion of Korah, Dathan and Abiram, or at least in response to it, we find the following passage:

> And the Lord said to Moses, 'Say to the congregation, Get away from about the dwelling of Korah, Dathan, and Abi'ram.' Then Moses rose and went to Dathan and Abi'ram; and the elders of Israel followed him. And he said to the congregation, 'Depart, I pray you, from the tents of these wicked men, and touch nothing of theirs, lest you be swept away with all their sins.' So they got away from about the dwelling of Korah, Dathan, and Abi'ram; and Dathan and Abi'ram came out and stood at the door of their tents, together with their wives, their sons, and their little ones. And Moses said, 'Hereby you shall know that the

Lord has sent me to do all these works, and that it has not been of my own accord. If these men die the common death of all men, or if they are visited by the fate of all men, then the Lord has not sent me. But if the Lord creates something new, and the ground opens its mouth, and swallows them up, with all that belongs to them, and they go down alive into Sheol, then you shall know that these men have despised the Lord.' And as he finished speaking all these words, the ground under them split asunder; and the earth opened its mouth and swallowed them up, with their households and all the men that belonged to Korah and all their goods. So they and all that belonged to them went down alive into Sheol; and the earth closed over them, and they perished from the midst of the assembly. And all Israel that were round about them fled at their cry; for they said, 'Lest the earth swallow us up!' And fire came forth from the Lord, and consumed the two hundred and fifty men offering the incense.   (Numbers 16:23–35)

In this story the focus is clearly on human rebellion, one that eventually includes the whole people a little later. But what I want to emphasize is the way human rebellion becomes one with natural chaos – in this case the earth opens up and swallows the rebels up. As with the Flood story, the 'earthquake' is an agent of punishment in the hands of a white terror God, but as with the Flood, it threatens to get out of control all too quickly. The people run for fear of their lives, lest they too should be swallowed up. Instead, a fire arbitrarily emerges and cooks a few hundred incense bearers.

The story of the Flood and the rebellion of Korah are just two examples of a theme that recurs time and again in the mythology of the Bible: political opposition, the threat of all and sundry against the powers that be, is cast as chaos in its mythology – so much so that human rebellion is followed by a barely controlled natural chaos as some form of punishment. In fact, I would argue that the desperate effort to overcome chaos is at one and the same time a desperate effort to overcome the threat of revolution. And it is this theme that a political myth of the worldly left might wish to consider reappropriating, for the theme of rebellious chaos is certainly worth a place in any political myth of the left.

There are of course more texts like this that may be retrieved from the Bible for a worldly left, but I have discussed a few to provide a picture of what such a political myth might look like. Some features, such as the condemnation of oppression and images of a communist society, have inspired the religious left in its earlier phases, and indeed many aspects of the old secular left in revised and secularized forms. What is different about my suggestions, at least in terms of the condemnations and images, is that any political myth requires a persistent theological suspicion in order to maintain an awareness of the ways they can become objects of worship in their own way, whether those objects are leaders or groups, or indeed paradises in the past that need to be restored. Nor should they become blueprints in their own right, for they are, after all, various strands of myth.

Conclusion

The Bible may well be 'rescued' by a resurgent worldly left, it seems to me. That worldly left arises in the context of the disintegration of the old programme of secularism. In its place I have suggested we think of a 'new secularism', one that sees the entwinement of religion and secularism as beneficial rather than a problem. And within that new secularism a worldly left may arise, one that brings together without homogenizing the various elements of the old secular left and the religious left, especially in a context where the left is in resurgence. The Bible is, however, a multi-valent and multi-vocal text, one that the political and religious right can use with ease to justify their agenda, but one that the worldly left can also use. Given this multi-valency, I argued for a redefinition of what the abuse of the Bible is, and suggested that it is any use of the Bible to justify and perpetrate the degradation and exploitation of people for whatever reason, whether that is in terms of class, ethnicity, gender, sexuality, species and so on. That type of use of the Bible to abuse needs to be relentlessly uncovered and condemned. However, a more viable use of the Bible appears where it is used to overcome such degradations, and I picked up a few elements in a rich history of the revolutionary use of the Bible. In particular, it seems to me that the Bible may well provide some elements of a political myth for a worldly left, for it is itself a profoundly mythical collection of texts. But it is one that should be read with a large helping of theological suspicion.

Notes

Chapter 1 The New Secularism

1 We still find the argument that secularism in the modern world is concerned with this age and not with any eschatology in the influential work of Hans Blumenberg (1966) and Karl Löwith (1949).

2 In this respect I am taking sides in an old debate. Within the English secularist movement a split opened up at the end of the nineteenth century between those, like George Holyoake, who argued that secularism should be indifferent to religion, that it was irrelevant, and those like Charles Bradlaugh, who argued that anti-religious activism was crucial to secularism. I think Holyoake was on the right track by arguing that secularism is not the same as atheism.

3 London Metropolitan University's 'Centre for Postsecular Studies' defines post-secularism in a slightly different fashion: 'A postsecular society is one with a renewed interest in the spiritual life. It is postsecular rather than presecular because it renews the inquiry into the spiritual life by building on the hard-won rights and democratic freedoms of expression in the secular world' (see www.jnani.org/postsecular/index.htm). Obviously there is agreement with my point concerning spiritualities, but I find it strange to associate 'rights and democratic freedoms' with secularism.

4 As Yvonne Sherwood notes, 'the "secular" and the "biblical" are not as alienated from one another as popular wisdom would have us believe' (Sherwood 2000: 201), and, '… the secular plays out its concerns and its disaffections *within the forum of the biblical text*' (Sherwood 2000: 203).

5 De Sade is famous for his quip in the context of the French Revolution, 'Frenchmen, one more effort' (*Français, encore un effort*) – all for the sake of the Sadean utopia where everything goes.

6 In fact, the last person to be convicted in England under the British Witchcraft Act was the clairvoyant Helen Duncan. She was convicted in 1944, although

she was not executed. Instead she spent nine months in prison so that she would not reveal the plans for the D-Day invasion of Europe through her clairvoyant powers. Only in 1951 was the British act repealed. One can't help wondering whether the walls of a prison cell would really cramp a clairvoyant's style.

Chapter 2 The Worldly Left: Towards a Politics of Alliance

1 Giorgio Agamben has offered a sustained analysis of this process, developing the concepts of 'state of exception' and 'bare life' in order to describe what is going on (Agamben 1998, 2005b).
2 See Alain Badiou on the bankruptcy of parliamentary democracy under capitalism (Badiou 2002: 98–9, 2003a: 78).
3 The League of the Just, a worldwide communist movement based on religious ideas, was the organization Marx and Engels joined before its name was changed to 'The Communist League'. See further Chapter 6, p. 130.

Chapter 3 Bad Conscience: Battles Over the Bible

1 The organization of chapters and verses in the English translation of this part of the book of Numbers differs from that of the Hebrew original.
2 This is a constant theme of the Murmuring Stories. Who murmurs? It is 'the people' in Exodus 15:24 and 17:3; 'the people of Israel' in Exodus 16:12, Numbers 14:27, 17:5 (Hebrew text 17:20); 'all the people of Israel' in Numbers 14:2; 'all the congregation' in Numbers 14:36 and Joshua 9:18; 'the whole congregation of the people of Israel' in Exodus 16:2 and 9, Numbers 16:11 (Hebrew text 17:6).
3 Reconstructions of the canonization of the Bible continue to appear at a steady pace (as a sample, see Sundberg 1964, Brettler 1994, Carr 1996, Davies 1998 and Aichele 2001). The status of the debate is covered rather well in McDonald and Sanders (2002), but they all operate within certain limits. They oscillate within three oppositions: diversity versus unity, conflict versus consensus, and rupture versus organic or evolutionary development. If you begin from the side of unity and consensus, then the problems arise with diversity and conflict, and vice versa. Often such reconstructions come up with ingenious and overlapping combinations of these three oppositions, with, for instance, an organic development broken by a rupture or two, or a consensus as the resolution of conflict, or a final unity out of diversity that is yet plagued by diversity. The dates vary between the supposed time of Ezra and Nehemiah (6th century BCE), through the era of the Hasmoneans (3rd to 2nd century BCE) to the rabbinic efforts in the first centuries of the Common Era. But dates, like the fashion in jeans, can go in one of two directions – up or down.

153

4 However, calling one text a 'forgery' and the others not – whether inside or outside the canon – is perhaps too fine a distinction. How many texts squarely in the canon – the books attributed to Moses, for instance, or the Pseudo-Pauline epistles – would not count as forgeries?

5 Not to mention the Epistle to the Laodiceans and 3 Corinthians, both of which were attributed to Paul and almost made it into the canon.

6 The Mabo decision of 1992 overturned the legal fiction of *terra nullius* which denied indigenous peoples any sense of ownership of the land. But establishing 'native title' has proven extremely difficult. After Mabo, it was thought that pastoral leases extinguished native title. However, the Wik decision (1996) showed that it was possible for both native title and pastoral leases to coexist. In 2002, the issue was further clarified when the High Court rejected an application for native title by the Yorta Yorta people, noting that indigenous groups must prove a 'substantially uninterrupted' traditional link to the land to establish native title. Most recently, the Noongar people became the first Aboriginal group successfully to claim native title with the Federal Court ruling (September 2006) that they are the traditional owners of the city of Perth. However, the Western Australia government is currently appealing the decision.

7 Honour where honour is due: I would like to thank Todd Penner for making this point in a personal communication.

Chapter 4 (Ab)using the Text: Conflicts in Politics and Science

1 The Liberal Party in Australia attempts to combine liberal or pro-market economic policies with a conservative social agenda, much like the Republicans in the USA, although there are some lone individuals in Australia who hold to the ideals of small 'l' liberalism. Unfortunately, in that strange country between Canada and Mexico the word 'liberal' has been distorted beyond recognition to refer to the left, especially in the combination 'left-liberal'. Of course, it is also a reflection of the parlous state of politics in the aforementioned country.

2 Facing the decline of religious observance in England, many social observers in the nineteenth century worried over the supposed loss of moral fabric.

Chapter 5 Making All Things New: The Revolutionary Legacy of the Bible

1 The texts are as follows: *The Mysterie of God concerning the whole Creation, Mankind* (1648); *The Breaking of the Day of God* (20 May 1648); *The Saints Paradise* (ca. 1648); *Truth Lifting up its Head above Scandals* (1649); *The New Law Of*

Righteousness (26 January 1649); *The True Levellers Standard ADVANCED: or, The State of Community opened, and Presented to the Sons of Men* (20 April 1649); *A DECLARATION FROM THE Poor oppressed People OF ENGLAND, DIRECTED To all that call themselves, or are called Lords of Manors, through this NATION* (1 June 1649); *A LETTER TO The Lord Fairfax, AND His Councell of War, WITH Divers Questions to the Lawyers, and Ministers: Proving it an undeniable Equity, That the common People ought to dig, plow, plant and dwell upon the Commons, with-out hiring them, or paying Rent to any. On the behalf of those who have begun to dig upon George-Hill in Surrey* (9 June 1649); *A Declaration of The bloudie and un-christian acting of William Star and John Taylor of Walton* (22 June 1649); *An Appeal To the House of Commons* (11 July 1649); *A Watch-Word to the City of London, and the Armie* (26 August 1649); *To His Excellency the Lord Fairfax and the Counsell of Warre* (December 1649); *To My Lord Generall and his Councell of Warr* (8 December 1649); *Several Pieces gathered into one volume* (1650); *A New-yeers Gift FOR THE PARLIAMENT AND ARMIE: SHEWING, What the KINGLY Power is; And that the CAUSE of those They call DIGGERS* (1 January 1650); *Englands Spirit Unfoulded* (ca. February or March 1650); *A Vindication of those … called Diggers* (4 March 1650); *Fire in the Bush* (19 March 1650); *An Appeale to all Englishmen* (26 March 1650); *A Letter taken at Wellingborough* (March 1650); *An Humble Request, to the Ministers of both Universities, and to all Lawyers in every Inns-a-court* (9 April 1650); *Letter to Lady Eleanor Davies* (4 December 1650); *The Law Of Freedom in a Platform, or True Magistracy Restored* (1652).

Chapter 6 Rescuing the Bible

1   In fact, in the UK blasphemy is still a criminal offence, although no-one has been sent to prison for blasphemy since 1921 and the last prosecution under the law was Mary Whitehouse vs. *Gay News* in 1977.

2   No word has been quite as abused as 'freedom' in our own time, as we find in US imperialism that claims the word as its own through such slogans as 'freedom through firepower', and as we find in the champions of capitalism such as Milton Friedman and Friedrich Hayek, who have managed to distort the word by claiming that a market economy and political freedom go hand in hand.

3   Although it needs a good dose of theological suspicion, Catherine Keller's book, *The Face of the Deep* (2003), is a stunning theological engagement with chaos.

References

Abbott, Tony. 1994. First Speech to Parliament, 31 May 1994. Available from www. tonyabbott.com.au/news/article.aspx?ID=228. Accessed 14 January 2007.

Abbot, Tony. 1999. Notes for Australia Unlimited Conference – Bridging the Incentive Gap, 4 May 1999. Available from www.tonyabbott.com.au/news/article. aspx?ID=238. Accessed 14 January 2007.

Abbot, Tony. 2004. The Ethical Responsibilities of a Christian Politician, 16 March 2004. Available from www.tmc.org.au/Adelaide/McAuley.PDF. Accessed 14 January 2007.

Abbot, Tony. 2007. Why Our Christian legacy Gets an Each-Way Bet. *The Sydney Morning Herald*, 3 January. Available from www.smh.com.au/news/opinion/ why-our-christian-legacy-gets-an-eachway-bet/2007/01/02/1167500123294. html. Accessed 5 April 2007.

Adorno, Theodor W. 1973. *The Jargon of Authenticity*, translated by K. Tarnowski and F. Will. Evanston, IL: Northwestern University Press.

Agamben, Giorgio. 1998. *Homo Sacer: Sovereign Power and Bare Life*, translated by D. Heller-Roazen. Stanford, CA: Stanford University Press.

Agamben, Giorgio. 2005a. *The Time That Remains: A Commentary on the Letter to the Romans*, translated by P. Dailey. Stanford, CA: Stanford University Press.

Agamben, Giorgio. 2005b. *State of Exception*, translated by K. Attell. Chicago: The University of Chicago Press.

Aichele, George. 2001. *The Control of Biblical Meaning: Canon as a Semiotic Mechanism*. Lewisburg, PA: Trinity Press International.

American Association for the Advancement of Science (AAAS). 2002. AAAS Board Resolution on Intelligent Design Theory. Available from www.aaas.org/news/ releases/2002/1106id2.shtml. Accessed 5 April 2007.

Archer, Mike. 2005. Intelligent Design is Not Science. Available from www.science. unsw.edu.au/news/2005/intelligent.html. Accessed 7 October 2006.

References

Badiou, Alain. 2002. *Ethics: An Essay on the Understanding of Evil*, translated by P. Hallward. London: Verso.

Badiou, Alain. 2003a. *Infinite Thought: Truth and the Return to Philosophy*, translated by J. Clemens and O. Feltham. London: Continuum.

Badiou, Alain. 2003b. *Saint Paul: The Foundation of Universalism*, translated by R. Brassier. Stanford, CA: Stanford University Press.

Behe, Michael J. 1996. *Darwin's Black Box: The Biochemical Challenge to Evolution*. New York: Free Press.

Belo, Fernando. 1981. *A Materialist Reading of the Gospel of Mark*, translated by M. J. O'Connell. Maryknoll, NY: Orbis.

Benjamin, Andrew. 2006. Israel Does Not Act or Speak for Every Jew. *The Sydney Morning Herald*, 4 August, p. 11. Available from www.smh.com.au/news/opinion/israel-does-not-act-or-speak-for-every-jew/2006/08/03/1154198265594.html. Accessed 5 April 2007.

Bloch, Ernst. 1972. *Atheism in Christianity: The Religion of the Exodus and the Kingdom*, translated by J. T. Swann. New York: Herder and Herder.

Bloch, Ernst. 1995. *The Principle of Hope*, translated by N. Plaice, S. Plaice and P. Knight, 3 vols. Cambridge, MA: MIT Press.

Blumenberg, Hans. 1966. *The Legitimacy of the Modern Age*, translated by R. M. Wallace. Cambridge, MA: MIT Press.

Boer, Roland. 2001. *Last Stop Before Antarctica: The Bible and Postcolonialism in Australia*. Sheffield, UK: Sheffield Academic Press.

Boer, Roland. 2007a. *Criticism of Heaven*, Historical Materialism Book Series. Leiden: E. J. Brill.

Boer, Roland. 2007b. *Political Myth*. Durham, NC: Duke University Press.

Boer, Roland. 2007c. Twenty Five Years of Marxist Biblical Criticism. *Currents in Biblical Research* 5 (3):1–25.

Boer, Roland, and Ibrahim Bahige Abraham. In press. Noah's Nakedness: Islam, Ethnicity and the Fantasy of the Christian West. In *Sacred Tropes: Tanakh, New Testament, Qur'an as Literary Works*, ed. R. Sabbath. Durham, NC: Duke University Press.

Bouma, Gary. 2006. Recipe Bringing Youth Back to Church. *The Sydney Morning Herald*, 28 February. Available from www.smh.com.au/news/opinion/many-flavours-one-size-is-recipe-bringing-youth-back-to-church/2006/02/27/1141020021815.html?page=fullpage. Accessed 5 April 2007.

Boyarin, Daniel, and Jonathan Boyarin. 1995. Diaspora: Generation and the Ground of Jewish Identity. In *Identities*, ed. K. A. Appiah and H. L. Gates Jr. Chicago: University of Chicago Press, pp. 305–37.

Brettler, Marc. 1994. How the Books of the Hebrew Bible Were Chosen. In *Approaches to the Bible: The Best of Bible Review, vol. 1: Composition, Transmission and Language*, ed. H. Minkoff. Washington, DC: Biblical Archaeology Society, pp. 108–12.

Broadway, Bill. 2001. War Cry from the Pulpit. *Washington Post*, 21 September, p. B09. Available from www.washingtonpost.com/ac2/wp-dyn?pagename=article&node=&contentId=A7059-2001Sep21. Accessed 5 April 2007.

Bush, George W. 2004. Remarks to the American Israel Public Affairs Committee, 18 May 2004. Available from www.state.gov/p/nea/rls/rm/32761.htm. Accessed 15 February 2006.

Carr, David M. 1996. Canonization in the Context of Community. In *A Gift of God in Due Season*, ed. R. D. Weis and D. M. Carr. Sheffield UK: Sheffield Academic Press, pp. 22–64.

Cone, James H. 1970. *A Black Theology of Liberation*. Maryknoll, NY: Orbis.

Costello, Peter. 2004. Address to National Day of Thanksgiving Commemoration Scots Church, 29 May 2004. Available from www.treasurer.gov.au/tsr/content/speeches/2004/007.asp. Accessed 21 August 2004.

Cunningham, Adrian, Terry Eagleton, Brian Wicker, Martin Redfern, and Lawrence Bright. 1966. *The Slant Manifesto: Catholics and the Left*. London: Sheed and Ward.

Davies, Philip R. 1998. *Scribes and Schools: The Canonization of the Hebrew Scriptures*. Louisville, KY: Westminster John Knox.

Davis, Percival, and Dean H. Kenyon. 1989. *Of Pandas and People: The Central Question of Biological Origins*. Dallas, TX: Haughton Publishing Company (Foundation for Thought and Ethics).

Dembski, William A. 1999. *Intelligent Design: The Bridge Between Science & Theology*. Downers Grove, IL: Intervarsity Press.

Dembski, William A. 2004. *The Design Revolution: Answering the Toughest Questions About Intelligent Design*. Downers Grove, IL: Intervarsity Press.

Docker, John. 2001. *1492: The Poetics of Diaspora*. London: Continuum.

Docker, John, and Ghassan Hage. 2003. Call for an Australian boycott of research and cultural links with Israel. *Borderlands* 2 (3), www.washingtonpost.com/ac2/wp-dyn?pagename=article&node=&contentId=A7059-2001Sep21. Accessed 5 April 2007.

Downer, Alexander. 2003. Speech at the Sir Thomas Playford Annual Lecture, 27 August 2003. Available from www.foreignminister.gov.au/speeches/2003030827_playford.html. Accessed 28 August 2003.

Eagleton, Terry. 1966. *The New Left Church*. London: Sheed and Ward.

Eagleton, Terry. 1970. *The Body as Language: Outline of a 'New Left' Theology*. London: Sheed and Ward.

Eagleton, Terry. 2003. *After Theory*. New York: Basic Books.

References

Exum, J. Cheryl. 2005. *Song of Songs: A Commentary*. Louisville, KY: Westminster John Knox.

Farouque, Farah. 2006. Howard Wants to See the Back of Burqa. *The Age*, 28 February, p. 3. Available from www.theage.com.au/news/national/howard-wants-to-see-the-back-of-burqa/2006/02/27/1141020024463.html. Accessed 5 April 2007.

Friedman, Milton. 2002. *Capitalism and Freedom: Fortieth Anniversary Edition*. Chicago: University of Chicago Press.

Garnaut, John. 2006. Costello to Violent Muslims: Get Out. *The Sydney Morning Herald*, 24 February, p. 1. Available from www.smh.com.au/news/national/love-australia-or-leave-it-costello/2006/02/23/1140670205134.html. Accessed 5 April 2007.

Gottwald, Norman K. 1999 [1979]. *The Tribes of Yahweh*. Sheffield, UK: Sheffield Academic Press.

Gramsci, Antonio. 1992. *Prison Notebooks*, translated by J. A. Buttigieg and A. Callari, vol. 1. New York: Columbia University Press.

Gramsci, Antonio. 1996. *Prison Notebooks*, translated by J. A. Buttigieg. Vol. 2. New York: Columbia University Press.

Greene, David L. 2003. Bush Turns Increasingly to Language of Religion. *Baltimore Sun*, 10 February 2003. Available from www.commondreams.org/headlines 03/0210-06.htm. Accessed 5 April 2007.

Hamilton, Clive. 2004. Peter Costello Should Practise What He Preaches. *The Age*, 9 June, p. 19. Available from www.theage.com.au/articles/2004/06/08/1086460293197. html?oneclick=true. Accessed 5 April 2007.

Harding, Susan. 1994. Imagining the Last Days: The Politics of Apocalyptic Language. In *Accounting for Fundamentalisms*, ed. M. E. Marty and R. S. Appleby. Chicago: Chicago University Press, pp. 57–78.

Hardt, Michael, and Antonio Negri. 2004. *Multitude: War and Democracy in the Age of Empire*. New York: Penguin.

Harrill, Albert J. 2006. *Slaves in the New Testament: Literary, Social and Moral Dimensions*. Minneapolis, MN: Fortress Press.

Harvey, David. 2000. *Spaces of Hope*. Berkeley: University of California Press.

Hayek, Friedrich von. 1960. *The Constitution of Liberty*. Chicago: University of Chicago Press.

Horsley, Richard. 1989. *Sociology and the Jesus Movement*. New York: Crossroad Publishing Company.

Horsley, Richard. 1992. *Jesus and the Spiral of Violence: Popular Jewish Resistance in Roman Palestine*. Philadelphia, PA: Augsburg Fortress.

Horsley, Richard. 1995. *Galilee: History, Politics, People*. Philadelphia, PA: Trinity Press International.

159

References

Horsley, Richard. 1996. *Archaeology, History and Society in Galilee*. Philadelphia, PA: Trinity Press International.

Horsley, Richard (ed.). 1997. *Paul and Empire: Religion and Power in Roman Imperial Society*. Philadelphia, PA: Trinity Press International.

Horsley, Richard. 2002. *Jesus and Empire: The Kingdom of God and the New World Order*. Minneapolis, MN: Augsburg Fortress.

Horsley, Richard. 2003. *Religion and Empire: People, Power, and the Life of the Spirit*. Minneapolis, MN: Augsburg Fortress.

Horsley, Richard, and John S. Hanson. 1985. *Bandits, Prophets, and Messiahs: Popular Movements in the Time of Jesus*. Philadelphia, PA: Trinity Press International.

Howard, John. 2005. PM's Christian Reflection. *The Age*, 26 December, p. 1. Available from www.theage.com.au/articles/2005/12/25/1135445476490.html?from=rss. Accessed 9 April 2006.

Kautsky, Karl. 1958. *Foundations of Christianity*, translated by H. F. Mins. London: Russell and Russell.

Keller, Catherine. 2003. *The Face of the Deep: A Theology of Becoming*. New York: Routledge.

Kristeva, Julia. 1987. *Tales of Love*, translated by L. S. Roudiez. New York: Columbia University Press.

Kristeva, Julia. 1991. *Strangers to Ourselves*, translated by L. S. Roudiez. New York: Columbia University Press.

Locke, John. 2003 [1689]. *Two Treatises of Government and A Letter Concerning Toleration*. New Haven, CT: Yale University Press.

Löwith, Karl. 1949. *Meaning in History: Theological Implications of the Philosophy of History*. Chicago: University of Chicago Press.

Löwy, Michael. 1996. *The War of Gods: Religion and Politics in Latin America*. London: Verso.

Luxemburg, Rosa. 1905. Socialism and the Churches. Available from www.marxists.org/archive/luxemburg/1905/misc/socialism-churches.htm. Accessed 20 October 2004.

Marx, Karl, and Friedrich Engels. 1967 [1848]. *The Communist Manifesto*. Harmondsworth, UK: Penguin.

Marx, Karl, and Friedrich Engels. 1975–2005. *Collected Works*, 50 vols. London: Lawrence & Wishart.

McDonald, Lee, and James A. Sanders. 2002. *The Canon Debate*. Peabody, MA: Hendrickson.

Meyer, Stephen C. 2002. The Scientific Status of Intelligent Design: The Methodological Equivalence of Naturalistic and Non-naturalistic Origins Theories. Centre for Science and Culture. Available from www.discovery.org/scripts/viewDB/index.php?command=view&id=1780. Accessed 7 October 2006.

References

Müntzer, Thomas. 1988. *The Collected Works of Thomas Müntzer*, translated by P. Matheson. Edinburgh: T & T Clark.

Neusner, Jacob. 1988. *The Mishnah: A New Translation*. New Haven, CT: Yale University Press.

Padget, Tim. 2006. Chavez: "Bush Has Called Me Worse Things". *Time*, 22 September. Available from www.time.com/time/world/article/0,8599,1538296,00.html. Accessed 5 April 2007.

Paley, William. 1809. *Natural Theology: or, Evidences of the Existence and Attributes of the Deity*, 12th edn. London: J. Faulder.

Pelosi, Nancy. 2003. Address to the American Israel Public Affairs Committee, 1 April 2003. Available from cosmos.ucc.ie/cs1064/jabowen/IPSC/articles/article0002405.html. Accessed 29 March 2007.

Pelosi, Nancy. 2005. Address to the American Israel Public Affairs Committee, 23 May 2005. Available from cosmos.ucc.ie/cs1064/jabowen/IPSC/articles/article0019430.html. Accessed 29 March 2007.

Rice, Condoleezza. 2005. Remarks at the American Israel Public Affairs Committee's Annual Policy Conference, 23 May 2005. Available from www.state.gov/secretary/rm/2005/46625.htm. Accessed February 15 2006.

Rudd, Kevin. 2006a. Faith in Politics. *The Monthly*, October. Available from www.themonthly.com.au/excerpts/issue17_excerpt_001.html. Accessed 5 April 2007.

Rudd, Kevin. 2006b. It's Time to Fight for the True Christian Principle of Compassion. *The Sydney Morning Herald*, 3 October. Available from www.smh.com.au/news/opinion/its-time-to-fight-for-the-true-christian-principle/2006/10/03/1159641321957.html. Accessed 5 April 2007.

Rudd, Kevin. 2006c. A Faith Short of Compassion. *The Sydney Morning Herald*, 9 November. Available from www.smh.com.au/news/opinion/a-faith-short-of-compassion/2006/11/08/1162661754059.html?page=fullpage. Accessed 5 April 2007.

Runions, Erin. 2004a. Biblical Promise and Threat in U.S. Imperialist Rhetoric, Before and After 9.11. *The Scholar and Feminist Online* 2 (2). www.barnard.columbia.edu/sfonline/reverb/runions1.htm

Runions, Erin. 2004b. Desiring War: Apocalypse, Commodity Fetish and the End of History. *The Bible and Critical Theory* 1 (1), DOI: 10.2104/bc040004, publications.epress.monash.edu/doi/abs/10.2104/bc040004.

Schubert, Misha. 2006. Howard Accused of Inflaming Tensions. *The Age*, 21 February, p. 5. Available from www.theage.com.au/news/national/howard-accused-of-inflaming-tensions/2006/02/20/1140284007959.html. Accessed 5 April 2007.

Sherwood, Yvonne. 2000. *A Biblical Text and Its Afterlives: The Survival of Jonah in Western Culture*. Cambridge, UK: Cambridge University Press.

References

Simon, Bob. 2002. Zion's Christian Soldiers. In *60 Minutes*. USA: CBS. Available from www.thefreelibrary.com/Zion's+Christian+soldiers:+the+%2260+minutes%22+transcript.+ (Special...-a094769715. Accessed 19 March 2007.

Smith, Richard, John Avery, Thomas Fardin, et al. 1650. A Declaration by the Diggers of Wellingborough – 1650. London: Giles Calvert. Available from www.rogerlovejoy.co.uk/philosophy/diggers/diggers3.htm. Accessed 5 April 2007.

Sneed, Mark. 2004. Qohelet and His 'Vulgar' Critics: A Jamesonian Reading. *Bible and Critical Theory* 1 (1): 1–12, DOI: 10.2104/bc040005, publications.epress.monash.edu/doi/abs/10.2104/bc040005

Sundberg, Albert. 1964. *The Old Testament of the Early Church*. Cambridge, MA: Harvard University Press.

Tadros, Edmund, and Jonathan Pearlman. 2006. Sydney Soldier Dies for Israel. *The Sydney Morning Herald*, 28 July 2006, p. 1. Available from www.smh.com.au/news/world/sydney-soldier-dies-for-israel/2006/07/27/1153816322388.html. Accessed 5 April 2007.

Taube, Jacob. 2004. *The Political Theology of Paul*. Stanford, CA: Stanford University Press.

Thaxton, Charles B., Walter L. Bradley, and Roger L. Olsen. 1984. *The Mystery of Life's Origin: Reassessing Current Theories*. New York: Philosophical Library Inc.

Wagner, Don. 2002. For Zion's Sake. *Middle East Report*, 223: 52–7.

West, Gerald. 1995. *Biblical Hermeneutics of Liberation: Modes of Reading the Bible in the Context of South Africa*, 2nd edn. Pietermaritzburg and Maryknoll, New York: Cluster and Orbis.

Winstanley, Gerrard. 1652. *The Law of Freedom in a Platform*. London. Available from www.bilderberg.org/land/lawofree.htm. Accessed 22 October 2006.

Winstanley, Gerrard, John Coulton, John Palmer, et al. 1649. *A Declaration From the Poor oppressed People of England, Directed To all that call themselves, or are called Lords of Manors, through this Nation*. Available from www.rogerlovejoy.co.uk/philosophy/diggers/diggers1.htm. Accessed 22 October 2006.

Winstanley, Gerrard, William Everard, Richard Goodgroome, et al. 1649. *The True Levellers Standard ADVANCED: OR, The State of Community Opened, and Presented to the Sons of Men*. Available from www.rogerlovejoy.co.uk/philosophy/diggers/diggers2.htm. Accessed 22 October 2006.

Žižek, Slavoj. 2000. *The Fragile Absolute, or, Why is the Christian Legacy Worth Fighting For?* London: Verso.

Žižek, Slavoj. 2001. *On Belief*. London: Routledge.

Žižek, Slavoj. 2003. *The Puppet and the Dwarf: The Perverse Core of Christianity*. Cambridge, MA: MIT Press.

Index of Subjects

Index of Biblical References

Old Testament

New Testament